101 WAYS TO SAVE MONEY
on Your
WEDDING

Barbara Cameron

adamsmedia
Avon, Massachusetts

Contains material adapted and abridged from *The Everything® Weddings on a Budget Book*,
2nd Edition, by Barbara Cameron, copyright © 2007 by F+W Publications, Inc.,
ISBN 10: 1-59869-418-9, ISBN 13: 978-1-59869-418-5.

Published by
Adams Media, an F+W Media Company
57 Littlefield Street, Avon, MA 02322. U.S.A.
www.adamsmedia.com

ISBN 10: 1-60550-632-X
ISBN 13: 978-1-60550-632-6

Printed in the United States of America.

J I H G F E D C B A

Library of Congress Cataloging-in-Publication Data
is available from the publisher.

This publication is designed to provide accurate and authoritative information with regard to
the subject matter covered. It is sold with the understanding that the publisher is not engaged in
rendering legal, accounting, or other professional advice. If legal advice or other expert assistance
is required, the services of a competent professional person should be sought.
—From a *Declaration of Principles* jointly adopted by a Committee of the
American Bar Association and a Committee of Publishers and Associations

Many of the designations used by manufacturers and sellers to distinguish their product are
claimed as trademarks. Where those designations appear in this book and Adams Media was aware
of a trademark claim, the designations have been printed with initial capital letters.

This book is available at quantity discounts for bulk purchases.
For information, please call 1-800-289-0963.

Contents

Contents

Introduction

Congratulations on your engagement! You're about to enter the exciting time of planning your dream wedding, and you may already have some of your biggest wedding wishes in mind. You might also be concerned about what this wedding is going to cost. You've heard the statistics. The average wedding costs over $25,000, and that's just the *average* wedding! Friends and family who have planned their own weddings recently may have struggled with their budgets, stressed about money, and perhaps even wound up eliminating some of their dream wedding elements. But this doesn't have to happen to you!

You might not be aware that there are many, many ways that you can plan your dream wedding for less money than you'd expect. All it takes is some insider information from the wedding industry, and you have that insider information right here in your hands! So you're going to find out how to make choices that can save you *50 percent* to *70 percent* off your purchases. You're going to find out where to search for the perfect wedding gown, sites, photographers, videographers, entertainers, and more. And you'll find out exactly how to time your searches to earn even bigger discounts.

When you follow the tips in this book, you may be able to get your dream wedding for half the price *or* get twice the wedding for your available budget! You won't have to sacrifice quality or the most important parts of your day, and you'll soon find that looking for bargains is actually *fun* . . . and can become a group activity when your friends and family help you find the perfect resources.

In the end, you'll achieve your dream wedding without any of your guests knowing where you cut corners, where you got creative, and where you made better choices for your budget. And most importantly, you'll be among the brides and grooms who *enjoy* their wedding planning process, because you won't be frightened or stressed about making expensive mistakes with your wedding planning. Warnings are included here to save you from the most common budget missteps.

Ready to start planning for less? Let's get started.

PART I

Your First Decisions

CHAPTER 1

Making a Budget

Which comes first, the wedding vision or the budget? That's entirely up to you! When building a wedding budget, as overwhelming as that can be, start with a vision of your dream wedding, and then make the financial decisions based on how to achieve that vision. You might want to look first at your available money, and then decide on the elements of the wedding based on what you can comfortably afford. When you're just starting out on your wedding plans, you will most likely find that wedding expenses are way more costly than you expected, and you may—at first—consider cutting some of your most wished-for wedding elements out of your big day. You would have loved to have a designer gown, for instance, but how could you possibly get one on such a modest budget? Before you make any decisions or rule any plan out of your wedding dream, start first with the big decisions that are going to shape your wedding planning experience. You may find that you have more money to work with than you thought—such as with parents' contributions—or that your partner agrees with you on not wanting a $5,000 wedding cake ... so you can certainly afford that designer gown now! These first few steps are designed to get you talking about your financial constraints and freedoms, your priorities, and who's going to help you bring your wedding dream to life.

1. Envision Your Wedding

Knowing what each of you wants is the first step in planning your wedding. Do you envision a big, formal wedding with a sea of roses, a five-course dinner, and an orchestra, or a more modest, informal outdoor wedding with you in a sundress holding a bouquet of wildflowers? Does your fiancé want a small wedding with just family? Or does he want to take the family off to Hawaii for a tropical fantasy wedding? Before you can make any wedding plans, and start to talk about paying for them, be sure you're united in your vision for the big day, or that you have mapped out where each of you will compromise your expectations to suit the other's wishes.

These steps will determine how and where you spend your money. Imagine what a relief it would be if both of you want an under-fifty-person guest list! Imagine how thrilling it would be when you both say, "Sit-down dinners aren't really what I have in mind" and realize that you can save 70 percent off the reception by planning a brunch or luncheon. It's only through discussing your wedding wishes that you can start the process off with big victories for your budget. You might begin thousands of dollars ahead of the game! That is, if you can agree on your wedding vision. Be prepared for wedding planning to require communication and compromise. It's a genuine team effort. So have a detailed discussion of how big a wedding you want, how formal, and any wished-for wedding elements, so that you can find beautiful ways to get those things for less.

Your smartest first step is to sit down together in front of your home computer and surf the Internet, visiting your favorite wedding websites and the sites for your favorite bridal magazines. Grooms say they enjoy looking at photos with their brides, and this initial evening of idea-hunting often turns into a few dozen printouts of reception styles, menu plans, wedding cake images, and other wedding vision–defining graphics. While looking at these photos and printing them out to show to your future vendors, take notes on what you want, what you don't want, where you can use an idea that's a no for him in another party such as your bridal shower, and also talk about what you saw and experienced at other weddings that you do or don't want for your own Big Day. Again, establish right now that you don't want the things other couples spend thousands of dollars on, like a sit-down dinner with lobster tails, filet mignon, and endless sushi bar, and a raw bar to rival most

Oscars™ parties. "No, that's so not for me!" will free you from the high-end menu and you'll also find out your partner agrees. That's the best way to start forming your realistic budget.

> **BRIDAL BONUS** In wedding budgets, there is the reception, and then there is everything else. The reception can cost up to 60 percent of the total budget. This includes the price of renting the reception hall or space itself as well as providing food and beverages for your guests.

2. Build Your Priority List

Ask yourselves which features of the wedding are important to you. Each of you should make a list of your most wished-for wedding elements and then star the two or three items that you feel are the most important to you, the ones you'd be willing to spend a larger chunk of your budget on. Is it the ceremony itself? The reception? The wedding dress? Flowers? Think about it. Star those high-priority items. Number them, if you wish to rank them further. And then compare your two lists to see how your priorities measure up. How closely do you and your fiancé agree on the big expenditures? Which two or three features matter most to you? Let's say you've picked the dress, the flowers, and the reception. Your fiancé is most concerned about the reception and the music. This means that as a couple, a team of equals, you have four top priorities where you'd like to invest more money and focus. These are the areas where you might not take the budget package, figuring you can save enough to balance out these higher expenses by taking the budget packages in invitations and other nonpriority areas. Your Priority List will show categories you can live without, such as a twelve-piece orchestra or limousines. Looking at your priority list, you get the instant thrill of crossing off some traditional wedding expenses from the basic checklists you found online, and seeing that you now have more money available for your top three or four choices.

WATCH OUT Check your lists to see whether you left off any potential wedding expenses. Omissions may point to areas that neither of you rate as a priority, which may turn into a 50 percent lower figure in that planning category. For instance, if neither of you mentioned the honeymoon, you can save money by opting for a less expensive locale. Hey, you can always get to Hawaii on your first wedding anniversary . . . especially without wedding stress, you'd probably have a much better time.

3. Give Yourselves Enough Time to Plan

While it is possible to plan a wonderful wedding, on a budget, in just a few months, the overriding wisdom in the wedding planning industry is that the more time you give yourselves, the better. According to TheWeddingReport.com, a national bridal survey website, the average length of today's engagements is fourteen months, giving the couple over a year to plan. And having that extra time often saves you a ton of money.

When you allow many months of planning, you give yourselves plenty of time to research each of your wedding vendors well, attend interviews with them, go see bands and deejays in action, visit many sites in order to choose the best ones for your ceremony and reception, attend bridal shows and expos to get exposed to the widest variety of experts in your area. You probably wouldn't buy a house in two months, right? You'd want to check out the market. As such, it's a wise move to set your wedding date for at least nine months from now and enjoy the entirety of that time researching your regional wedding opportunities and professionals together, even stopping in to take a quick look at an actual wedding taking place at a potential wedding site during the season you're considering for your wedding. This is very important! If you are thinking about a spring wedding date, this fourteen months of planning time will allow you to pop into a real-couple's spring wedding, see the grounds in bloom (and thus show you that you won't need to buy extra décor because the site is lush with planted tulips and cherry blossom trees), look at the colors and the food and the specialty drinks at the bar, the wedding cake. When you're researching during the season of your wedding, even though it's for the next calendar year, you'll discover a ton of insider secrets and creative new ideas (such as pretty spring flowers at the nursery) to bring big savings into your wedding.

Another plus is that you'll have plenty of opportunities to enjoy seasonal and holiday sales on many different kinds of materials such as décor items from the craft store, dresses, accessories, favors, and gifts. Throughout the year, you can take advantage of four to six seasonal and holiday sales with savings up to 70 percent, often more during the winter holiday shopping season.

If you don't give yourself enough time to plan, you may wind up spending a lot more money, booking last-minute at higher rates (a shady pro might think, "They're desperate!"), or rush through decisions and tasks at breakneck pace, often not making the smartest financial decisions.

WATCH OUT Keep in mind, wedding expenses are on the rise. Nearly every aspect of the wedding has increased more than 20 percent since 2002, according to CNNMoney.com. TheWeddingReport.com says that the average amount spent on a wedding is now at $29,614, up $2,000 in just two years, with similar increases projected for every year in the future. Looking at such dramatic price hikes from year to year, booking way in advance gives you a big financial advantage.

As an added plus, you can often "lock in" a vendor or site for their current year's pricing if you book at the end of the year, avoiding the price hike of the new calendar year's packages. Just be sure to get those terms stated in your contract, and you could save thousands of dollars just by booking early!

4. Working with Your Budget Team

Now it's time to get together with those involved in footing the bill. Is the bride's family paying or is the groom's? Are you, as a couple, paying for it yourselves? Many couples are getting married later these days, and they are financially secure enough to pay for their own wedding. They want to make decisions themselves without input or interference from parents. Today there are no rules for who pays.

Etiquette aside, you would be at a distinct advantage financially if you were able to include contributions from both your parents, and some couples are lucky enough to have grandparents offer to donate a few hundred or a few thousand dollars toward the big day. Parents and grandparents want to give you the day of your dreams, even if it's tough for them to spare such a large amount of money. Overall, it's quite common for a bride and groom to accept the help of parents and others, but with a few important ground rules to keep the windfall from causing greater problems than money shortages.

Remember that when others are helping to foot the bill, they usually feel they have something to say about how the money is spent. You and your fiancé have to carefully consider the hidden costs of accepting money if you feel there may be problems. Your wedding—and the planning that goes into it—is supposed to be a joyous occasion, not one fraught with controversy and conflict. So here are some tips to keep your parental cash-flow from causing problems:

- Explain to parents and others that while you're grateful for their generous help, you do have the plans for your wedding firmly in mind. You welcome their input along the way, but you are committed to having this day reflect your wishes as a couple.
- Make sure each financially involved party gives you a firm dollar amount that they plan to contribute. Hashing out details now might be uncomfortable, but it will save you from the anguish of a potentially disastrous misunderstanding later.
- Don't spend money you haven't received yet. Sometimes parents say they will give you $3,000, but unexpected expenses arise and they may have to lower that amount in the future. So never spend money you haven't yet received. Wait until their check clears. And never pressure parents to give as much as they promised originally. Just be grateful for what you do get, since you're very lucky to have financial help from parents when so many other couples do not have that luxury.

- If your family is paying, ask how much they are willing to spend. How flexible is their offer? Are they aware of what wedding expenses cost? Show them the website *www .costofwedding.com* so that they can see the average amounts spent on catering, photography, and many other categories in the region where you live. They need to make an informed estimate of how much money will realistically achieve your wedding goals.
- Let parents know that plans may change in the future. Can they adjust the amount for unforeseen expenses?
- Work out how your family will transfer the money to you and when it will be available. Will you receive a check? Will they transfer funds directly into your bank account? Will they pay the caterer or the florist directly? You need to understand the terms of these financial gifts so that you know what to expect.

You may have to choose your battles. If there are ongoing disagreements about how much they'll donate and how, decide what you absolutely must have and weigh it against your family's financial help. You may find that some things aren't as important as you thought, and that you can make a few changes to your plans without any anguish. Or, you might decide to split the cost of flowers with your parents so that you can get the arrangements you'd like. You'll just take a few hundred dollars away from another category to allow you to pay for more florals.

If you and your fiancé are paying for your own wedding, how will you make it work? You need to talk about where the money will come from, such as credit, your tax refund check, birthday gift money. Write down the sources of the money you personally can spend, which is a great way for you to keep each other from overspending with your credit cards. You may want to set up a joint account just for the wedding. Having a wedding-specific account will help you keep track of how much you have spent and how much you have left, when all of your expenses are listed in one place. Organization is a top key for saving money on your wedding.

BRIDAL BONUS More and more couples are paying for their own weddings. The latest studies show that 32 percent of couples now pay for their own nuptials. An estimated 30 percent of brides' parents pay for the wedding, according to Condé Nast Bridal Group.

5. Determining Your Budget

First, sit down and decide how much you can spend. That's your bottom figure. Then decide how much you could stretch that if you had to. Your budget must include a substantial cushion to cover any miscellaneous or unexpected expenses. Given your own sense of how much money is "a lot" as well as what you've read in magazines or heard from friends, determine which category your budget falls into: modest, moderate, or luxurious.

BRIDAL BONUS Visit *www.costowedding.com* to see the average expenses for every area of wedding plans in the region where you live. This national survey site will show you what other brides are spending on their gowns, invitations, favors, and all manner of bridal categories. You'll get a view of the average expenses in your area, knowing that many prices you'll find may be higher or lower depending on the vendors you visit. Again, some regions are more expensive than others, so look to this site to help you determine if it might be better for your budget for you to hold the wedding in your groom's hometown where everything costs 20 percent less, or perhaps in a destination location such as a beach or ski town an hour away. It might spell success for your budget if you look at other areas that are still close enough for you to drive to, offering you way more variety in sites and vendors, as you figure out your budget right now.

Of course, what these categories really mean will be different depending on which part of the country you're in and the locale of your wedding. For example, a budget some would consider moderate in Crossett, Arkansas, could be termed modest in Atlanta, Georgia. However, large cities may give you more options for a less expensive wedding. Small towns may have only one vendor for a wedding gown and one photographer. Be aware that you may incur additional expenses for travel time—either because you have to drive to a bigger city to find what you want or because you choose more distant vendors to come to you. The tricky thing about wedding budgets is that every bride and groom face unique challenges in their locations and the number of vendors and sites available to them. You might be lucky enough to live in an area where weddings are priced in a moderate range. If you live where weddings are extremely expensive, that just means you'll need to put more ideas from this book into action, and you'll be on the same footing as couples living in less expensive regions.

Think of your wedding budget as one of the first times you and your fiancé will discuss your attitudes about money, plan expenditures, and work together to execute your plan. It's the perfect place to lay a strong foundation for a successful financial union. Even if one of you is doing most of the planning and spending, it's important that you both agree on how this will be done. That spirit of budgetary responsibility will reflect itself in marital harmony.

Making your financial decisions—for the wedding and for life—through discussion, compromise, and sound budget principles will set you up for success. Apply these principles to your wedding expenses, and you will know what to expect for your financial future together.

What Is Your Money Personality?

It will help to know how you and your fiancé handle money and how your strategies differ. From there you can work together to find a way to handle your finances in a way that suits both of you. Most people are a combination of these personality types:

- *Impulsive Spender:* A stressful day at the office drives you to frivolous spending at the mall or an expensive dinner on the way home. You feel you work hard and deserve to have what you want. After all, you only live once.
- *Frugal (Non-)Spender:* Save, save, save! You adhere to the philosophy that you never know when you might need some extra cash. You find it hard to spend money, and you give every potential purchase so much thought that others squirm when they're out shopping with you.
- *Bingeing Consumer:* You save money for a long time, then go on a spending spree.
- *Ostrich:* You avoid thinking about money. You spend it but you don't keep a balanced checkbook, and you have made a few missteps that have cost you in late fees or other penalties.
- *Worrier:* You stress over your finances constantly. You are meticulous about organizing financial records, paying your bills on time, and keeping your checkbook balanced.

Before making a purchase for your wedding, ask yourself if you really need the item, or if you just want it. Make it a rule to think about it overnight and see how you feel the next day. As you build your budget, you'll need to come to terms with your financial personality as it meshes with your groom's. It may take an honest heart-to-heart to get you both to limit your spending or feel better about how you invest in the wedding. Again, communication is key. This is an important relationship-building time for you as well, so think about the budget not as a bad thing, but as an important lesson for you both.

6. Provide an Extra Expenses Fund

When creating your budget, looking at the amount you'll have available to spend, where it's coming from, and when you'll need it handy, be sure to create a category for "Extra Expenses" that will crop up during your planning season. You can't predict everything you'll experience throughout your talks with your vendors, and many brides and grooms experience rocky times with their budgets when they are told about extra fees, delivery charges, rental fees, site use fees, permits for parking at a beach, permits for alcohol consumption at a state park, and other unforeseen charges. There are even extra charges at some reception halls just for the serving staff to cut each piece of cake and put it on a plate. These unexpected charges can add up, pushing the uninformed bride and groom way over their budget. And you don't want to be the couple who has to go to your parents to ask for more money, right? You don't want your dad chastising you for not reading the fine print on a contract? Avoid all potential stresses by establishing your Extra Expenses fund, containing a few hundred dollars of "cushion cash," that you may have left over at the end of the wedding planning stage to use on your wedding day hairstyle or on a special dinner on your honeymoon.

BRIDAL BONUS Ask if you qualify for a discount whenever you're talking to a wedding vendor or site manager. There are discounts for students, senior citizens, AAA members, members of the military, alumni, and repeat customers. Your company or professional association might have a list of discounts for which you are eligible. Many companies offer their employees significant discounts, such as 20 percent to 50 percent off office supplies, photocopying, car rentals, even gym memberships! Check your company website or your Human Resources department to see which discounts you may be able to rack up.

Where do you put this Extra Expenses fund? It might be an envelope of cash you keep in your home safe so that you can't possibly tap into it through uncontrolled ATM withdrawals, or it might be a separate bank account that you set up for emergencies or for "play money" in the future. Right now, that account is for your Extra Expenses, which is a wise move to make to protect your budget in the future.

CHAPTER 2

Set the Foundation of Your Wedding Day

*I*t seems like common sense, but it really is vitally important to your wedding budget when you make the right foundational decisions, such as planning a smaller wedding rather than a three-hundred-person bash, choosing the right time of year, the right location, and other factors that can improve your wedding budget's power. When you make the smartest decisions in the upcoming categories, you can achieve twice the wedding for the same amount of money.

7. Determine the Size of Your Wedding

Considering that the largest portion of most wedding budgets goes to the reception, that means you're looking at significant charges per-person. So a fifty-person guest list is going to cost you more than that three-hundred-person bash. It's just basic math. That said, you don't have to eliminate most of your family and friends at great heartache and sacrifice. You can have a larger guest list, but find other ways to save throughout your planning. This topic is just something to keep in mind, since many couples and parents do get tempted to invite way too many people to the wedding. If you're on a budget, that might not be possible.

So establish your guest list count with an eye toward your budget, perhaps limiting guest lists on both sides of the family to a set total of one hundred people tops. Make sure all planning team members are aware of your limitations and this important set figure so that you avoid budget strains when someone goes overboard and invites all the third cousins.

During the months of planning, it's important to stick to a set number of guests and not let the guest list mushroom, because that will make your total expenses rise. Parents may need to be reminded a few times, since they are the most common offenders to the rule. "Just six more people" leads to sixty more people. "They'll be offended if we don't invite them" is a common parental complaint, often guilting brides and grooms into enlarging the guest list.

If your guest list is getting out of hand, put the brakes on it quickly. Separate your guests into two categories, A and B. The A list contains your parents, siblings, and other guests who absolutely must attend. The B list contains coworkers, extended family, and guests whom it would simply be nice to invite. You might want to create a more detailed Tiers List, with an A, B, C, and D breakdown, making it easy for you to eliminate all the Ds for a quick chop of sixty extra guests.

This isn't easy to do, since so many people will want to attend your wedding, and it's often one of the toughest experiences in wedding planning. Take a deep breath and remember what's important here. Your wedding day is all about celebrating your special day with the people you care about and who care about you. So the people you don't know shouldn't be on the list. Parents' friends may have to be cut from the list. Kids may not be able to be invited, eliminating another thirty names from the list.

WATCH OUT Never invite guests thinking that they'd never be willing to fly in to attend the wedding, but they'll send a gift anyway. Most couples find that faraway relatives and friends do accept wedding invitations since they haven't seen everyone in so long. That can add a large number of extra guests to the list, at great expense.

When it really comes down to it, no one wants to see you bankrupt or stressed because of the wedding or the reception. Guests who inquire about the wedding will have to be told, "We're sorry, but we chose to keep our guest list small due to space and budget constraints." They will just have to accept that they aren't invited to this particular wedding in the family. It's a necessity, and it was a tough decision for you.

8. Set the Wedding Date

You may be able to save a significant amount of money if you have the flexibility to schedule your wedding (or even just the honeymoon) during the off-peak season. The wedding industry has a peak season, usually extending from May to September, during which expenses may be higher due to supply and demand. In the great weather, more weddings take place, and families will be willing to pay higher amounts to hold the wedding during that time. Off-season dates during January through April and October through December, often find prices lowered by vendors who aren't so busy and want to attract your business. In some areas, an April wedding can cost one-third the price of a September wedding! That adds up to savings of thousands of dollars for the exact same wedding! So consider if a spring or winter wedding would fit your vision, especially since those dates are so budget-friendly.

Remember, though, that some holidays such as New Year's Eve and Valentine's Day do fall within off-season months, but they are among the most expensive times just because of the celebratory or sentimental nature of the holiday. So expect to see higher prices at that time, and perhaps avoid those holidays.

Vendors may be willing to negotiate with you for lower fees in off-peak months. You will also enjoy less crowded conditions at wedding and honeymoon venues, which can add the extra perk of more personalized service, more privacy, and sometimes freebies that vendors throw in because they want to impress your guests, who may become future clients of theirs! Off-season weddings do extend these kinds of perks.

As you plan your date, ask yourselves how important the month and even the day of the week is to you. If you are having a small wedding and most of your guests are local, a Friday evening or Sunday afternoon wedding could work well. These off-peak times can save you 10 to 30 percent off your wedding expenses, since a vendor or site can book you as the third wedding they're working that weekend. To entice you to book with them, they often slice their prices, which benefits you! Some couples whose guests are all local will even book their weddings for a Tuesday or Wednesday night for even greater savings, sometimes as much as 50 percent off!

Finally, think about the time of day for your wedding. An eight o'clock evening wedding is traditionally ultraformal and thus ultraexpensive. A six o'clock evening wedding will require dinner to be served, which creates higher expenses for a cocktail party and a dinner for your guests. If you hold an afternoon formal wedding, though, which can still include a cocktail party and seated meal, you might spend 20 percent less for a reception that's almost identical to the pricey late-night menu. Hotels and banquet halls price their packages according to time of day and type of meal, so perhaps a morning or afternoon wedding would be best for your budget. Don't worry about disappointing your guests when you don't serve a dinner. If you make the right choices with your menu, they'll be equally pleased with luncheon or brunch dishes, and you save a fortune. Check out the chapter on reception catering for some inspiring ideas that might lead you to make the foundational decision to time your wedding earlier in the day.

> **WATCH OUT** Check with your local chamber of commerce or visitor's bureau to learn whether there are any big events scheduled during the week of your wedding. This will ensure that your guests don't have a difficult time finding rooms or have to pay dramatically marked-up rates. In addition, check with the hotel most guests will be staying at to make sure it can accommodate your guests. Hotels with conference centers often fill up with business clients, especially if there is a large corporate event scheduled.

9. Decide on the Location

The location of the wedding, as you read earlier, can affect the budget tremendously. How are the rates in your hometown?

In your groom's? Your parents'? His parents'? What are the prices for the nice neighborhood just a half hour away from your home? What about in a nearby tourist town with lots of attractions? Do a bit of research to see if moving your wedding to another town will allow you to save money on all the elements of your day. This is where a wedding coordinator can be of great help to you, knowing surrounding areas very well. You may be able to save yourselves thousands of dollars by choosing the right setting for your wedding.

And here's something to keep in mind. When it's hot in your hometown in June, it might be cool and off-season at a destination site. So always think globally when deciding on the location for your wedding.

Another factor is your guests. It's almost certain that at least a few of your guests will be traveling to the wedding from out of town. Some couples pay for out-of-town guests' transportation and lodging, but this is entirely up to you. Travel expenses may include not only the airfare and hotel, but also the taxi, shuttle, or rental-car charges. It is a nice gesture and a good way to ensure your loved ones will be able to be there for your day, but it is expensive, especially for a couple on a strict budget. Fortunately, there are many ways for you to lessen the financial impact on your guests.

- Give them info. At the very least, provide your guests with the names and phone numbers of local hotels, motels,

airlines, and transportation companies. This is a helpful money- and time-saving service that your guests will
appreciate.

- Research hotel rates. Whether you choose to pay for all of
their expenses or not, you still need to provide your guests
with information and options. You can arrange for special
hotel rates for your wedding party, especially if you are
using a particular hotel for your reception. Discounted
room-block rates can save you 10 percent or more on rooms
booked by your guests, with no financial investment on your
part. You just arrange for a discount room block, and your
guests do the rest.

- Ask the hotel sales manager to arrange for free shuttle service to and from the airport for your guests.

- Don't forget that an experienced travel agent can be a good
resource for you and your guests, finding terrific moderately priced hotels and travel deals.

- Use your own expertise with discount travel websites such
as Orbitz to find great deals.

- Ask if guests can use their AAA discounts or other savings
plans when they book, and share this information with them.

- Select a place that is close to the ceremony and reception
sites to cut down on the expenses of taxi or rental-car use to
get guests from one place to another.

- Ask whether the hotel will honor the discounted rate for
guests who want to extend their visit a few days before or

after the wedding. Make certain the wedding party and other guests know they must ask for the special rate by requesting the "Smith wedding party rate." Some hotels make it easy on you and your guests, creating a personalized website for you that your guests can visit to book hotel rooms directly.

- Offer a Plan B. Be aware that while a hotel may be a wonderful location for your reception, its rooms might be pricey for some of your guests, especially if the week of your wedding is during peak season.

Have a few alternate choices you can offer those who need information on a place to stay. Some hotel reservation sites enable you to take a virtual tour of their rooms without leaving your home computer, but it's always best for you to take an in-person tour to be sure the hotel is clean and acceptable for your guests.

- Look into travel deals for wedding groups. American Airlines offers special discounts for wedding guests. If ten or more guests fly American Airlines to get to your wedding, they are eligible for a 5-percent savings on the lowest applicable airfare if you sign up for the discount.
- Don't be in airfare denial—sometimes the longer you wait, the steeper the price. Airfares might zoom astronomically during certain times of the year—or seats might be totally

unavailable. Remind guests to tie down their airline reservations. No one needs to pay extra because they waited to make reservations and your city hosted the NBA Finals the week of your wedding!

- Look into rental cars.

> **WATCH OUT** When you're newly engaged and not yet mired in the depths of wedding expenses, you might be overly excited about the wedding plans and tell your bridal party that you'll pay for their travel and lodging, and some of them may take you up on your offer, agreeing to be in the bridal party because it's not going to cost them an arm and a leg. Months later, you can't take the offer back, and there you are with thousands of dollars of racked-up expenses you could have avoided. Be generous instead by finding them lower-priced hotel rooms or suggesting a bed-and-breakfast for them all to stay at. Visit *www.BnBFinder.com* to find budget-friendly and charming B&Bs in your area.

Many of the large rental-car companies offer group discounts to wedding guests. Getting discounted rates for your guests might require a little effort on your end, but it's a welcome break to offer your guests, or to enjoy yourselves! Go to the rental-car website and submit a customer-service query or call the customer service number. You will receive a discount code to pass along to your guests. The discount varies depending on which size vehicle each guest reserves.

10. Working with a Wedding Coordinator

With everything you have to do, it may be worth the financial investment to have as many arrangements and details as possible taken care of by others. The basic strategy is one of delegation, and you can save a fortune by hiring a wedding coordinator to guide you through all or part of your wedding plans. These experts have detailed knowledge of every site and every vendor in the area, so they can suggest the best-priced plans and sites for your budget, and steer you away from bad deals and inexperienced vendors. Keep in mind that good consultants usually have working relationships with excellent vendors and venues that can translate into opportunities for savings. Some consultants establish partner savings plans and discounts with various florists and photographers, tux shops and entertainers with whom they work often, which can hand a big discount to you. Just be sure to research these recommended pros well, and interview them on your own to be sure you're getting the best expert at the best price.

Some consultants charge a flat fee; others charge a percentage of the wedding budget (typically 10 to 15 percent). Many couples find that this expense is well worth it when a coordinator's advice and connections save them thousands of dollars, so it's money well spent. Be sure to clarify fees before you make a final decision about the person you hire, but don't base your decision on the fee alone. Consider how much you plan on having the consultant do for you. Some can be hired just to find your sites, some just to find your vendors, some to run things on the wedding day so that you don't have to worry or work, and some will handle everything throughout the entire process. You get to decide which plan works best for you.

Ask your prospective wedding consultant about her experience. Some people take special courses; others use the term loosely to describe themselves when they only want to sell you their very own goods or services. Depending on the amount of work you'll have the consultant do for you, you may not need someone with professional training, so be clear on what services you actually need.

Sure, you could save money by doing most things for your wedding yourself. But do you really want to be up late the night before your ceremony affixing flowers to a wedding canopy, writing out a seating chart, and folding napkins into swans? Not only will you look stressed and haggard the next day, you will feel it, and you'll miss out on enjoying the perfect experience you've both worked so hard to create.

Some wedding consultants provide rental items for a wedding and reception, such as candleholders, chairs, and vases. Do some comparison shopping to price these items in advance so you know you're not being overcharged. It's a sign of good wedding consumerism when you invest your time to check out pricing on the Internet and through calls to various resources. A great wedding coordinator can save you money, but it's always best to be your own advocate and not depend on any other person in these cases. Some brides and grooms do find better-priced deals through their own research, and they simply tell their coordinator to acquire services through the site or store they just found.

> **BRIDAL BONUS** The best wedding consultants have completed training and certification to become certified wedding consultants. Information on what to look for if you're interested in hiring a wedding consultant is on the Association of Certified Professional Wedding Consultants website, *www.acpwc.com*, as well as through the Association of Bridal Consultants at *www.bridalassn.com*. Here, you'll find a list of the accredited wedding coordinators in your area, and you can interview them through free consultations to inspect their price packages and judge if they would be great to work with.

Whenever you investigate wedding coordinators, be sure you get a list of references and call them. Talk to former clients and find out whether the consultant did all she was supposed to do. Also, take the time to get a feel for the wedding consultant so you can determine whether she will provide the style and quality of service you want.

If you don't hire a wedding consultant but would still like some extra assistance, remember that reception sites such as hotels also have event planners who can help a good deal in planning your wedding and reception. They know their sites inside and out, and they can be invaluable in deciding on the timing of every last detail. So this might be a great, free way to get insider help to save you money as you plan.

11. Approach and Interview Vendors

For every element of your wedding, you will deal with experienced professionals who offer their services in price packages ranging from the platinum package to the budget package, with different levels of service in each. You will need to know the best ways to approach and communicate with these vendors to get the best-priced deals and the elements you want for your day.

> **BRIDAL BONUS** Recently, some couples have arranged to list their vendors' names on the back of their wedding programs in exchange for free goods, services, or a concession in price. They pay next to nothing for their wedding day in exchange for their services, since the experts get to "advertise" to all of the guests by virtue of showing their pretty floral arrangements or gorgeous wedding cake.

Bear in mind that many experts are perfectly willing to discuss your wishes for a budget wedding, and tailor their plans to suit your needs. You're not always stuck with the items listed on their price lists. You may be able to negotiate better deals for yourself. If you've never bargained with a salesperson or vendor, now is the time to learn that negotiating is an acceptable practice and can be beneficial for all involved. Often, vendors would rather compromise on a price than lose the sale.

How you approach a vendor can result in successful savings on options. For example, you could offer to have a friend pick up the cake to save on a delivery fee, if that's possible.

Negotiating is all about options: defining what you want, what you want to pay for what you want, and what you want to do if you don't get what you want.

It's very simple. Negotiating is about personal power, self-control, and sticking to your ultimate goal—saving on everything you can so you have the money for the special things you desire.

What many people don't realize is that shopkeepers and vendors are very often willing to negotiate on price. Veteran shoppers of antique fairs, flea markets, and other places where bargains abound will tell you that vendors feel very vulnerable when the flow of customers slows and their merchandise isn't moving. So that gives you the power, especially during off-peak wedding months, to negotiate fairly and earn yourself great discounts.

Part of the skill of negotiating lies in asking. You never know what you can get until you ask. Basically, there are two possible answers: yes and no. We've all dealt with rejection and lived through it, so know that if your offer is rejected you won't suffer a humiliating fate. Politely thank the vendor and move on.

The Negotiating Technique

Here is a simple way to negotiate. Approach the shopkeeper or vendor when she is not hassled by too many customers at once. If you notice she has just had an unpleasant conversation with a customer before you, use this to your advantage by smiling sympathetically and being extra courteous in your request.

Explain your situation—for example, that there is a stain on a dress you are interested in buying and you would like to get a discount on this damaged product. If it's an item that is dangerously out-of-season, like a swimsuit at the end of the summer or a summer wedding gown that is still on the rack long past the time a bride could wear it without shivering, then you should mention that fact. Have an idea in your head of how much you would like to see the item discounted. If the shopkeeper agrees, you've just saved yourself some money.

If you're not sure whether you can negotiate, practice with a friend until you feel more confident. It's a skill that will come in handy when you want a lower price from a caterer or a better deal on a honeymoon package.

If you receive a quote that isn't a bargain, express regret and name the amount you were hoping the price would be, adding that it will take *X* amount of time and money to make this item something you can use. If the item is expensive, be sure to mention that you are spending a lot of money. Also point out if you are a frequent customer.

If you don't get what you want a second time, ask very politely if there is anyone more senior who could authorize a price adjustment. If there is not an adjustment at this point, politely express regret, shake your head, and say that you're sorry, you just won't be able to take it. Turn and prepare to return the item to the rack or shelf. If you're with someone, say you guess you're just going to have to look elsewhere, so you'd both better be leaving now.

See what happens when you do this—you may well hear, "Wait, let me see what I can do," as you turn your back. Be gracious as they make another offer and see if you are happy with that. If not, decide whether you want the item or want to continue shopping.

Once you've tried this negotiating technique and had success, you'll never want to pay full price again. Remember, the issue is not whether you're able to spend the money, it's that you don't want to. You'd rather spend the money you save on something else.

Bartering

If you have a skill or product that you can trade for something you want, take advantage of it. Bartering is, simply put, exchanging things rather than paying for them with money.

I have something you want, and you have something I want, so we can exchange those things instead of paying each other. Why is this good? It's simple: Neither of us necessarily has money to pay for those things we want, but we have items we can trade for them.

The key to bartering is that the services or goods traded must be of equal value. You might be experienced with creating websites and can offer to create one in exchange for something a shopkeeper or vendor has to offer you. Perhaps the venue that will host your reception looks like it needs a service like painting or decorating, which you or your fiancé do. Not only might you save money on goods and services for your wedding, you might get some nice publicity or future business from the bartering opportunity.

Think about whether there is an opportunity and explore it mentally before you approach the other person so that you will be prepared to negotiate the barter. Use the same technique as for negotiating—except that instead of asking for a discount, you are offering to trade a service—or, if a complete swap of the item or service isn't possible, you can ask for a barter with some cash still exchanging hands. If you have a business card, you can always leave it with the shopkeeper or vendor so that he can think about your offer. This too is a way that many couples are wisely earning some of their wedding goods and services for free, or at least knocking a good percentage of the price down.

12. Get Smart about Contracts

As a smart, educated consumer—particularly with something as important as your wedding—you must pay great attention to the legalities of all of your wedding purchases and orders. Keep the following actions in mind as you work with each and every one of your vendors:

- Remember to get every business transaction in writing. This cannot be stressed enough. You don't want to have to put down additional deposits when you find that your arrangements have fallen through. Too much is at stake to rely on verbal assurances. As a matter of organization, you will be happy to see your records of when payments were made, and you might avoid paying double when a confused clerk sends you a duplicate bill.
- Write everything down. When you arrange for a service, write down the name of the person you talked to, the date when you spoke, and the order plans, just to be sure you have all of the details correct, and so that you can correct any confusion with your order in the future. Couples who don't do this can sometimes get ripped off and pay double.
- Read the fine print. If there are extra charges listed on the contract, ask for them to be removed if they are not what you agreed to. Most vendors will happily remove them.

- Don't rush into signing a contract before you read it. It's okay to ask to take the contract home so that you can read it fully, and at your leisure. It's a bad idea to just sign a paper put in front of you to get it done.
- Never agree to work with a vendor who doesn't offer a written contract. Just walk away.
- Use a credit card. First and foremost, you will have more consumer recourse if something goes wrong than if you pay with a check. Second, you may also reap the benefits of points, air miles, or other promotional programs. Your honeymoon is the perfect opportunity to take advantage of such perks, so call your credit card company and see what they have available. Be sure to read the terms and conditions thoroughly. To take full advantage of this money-saving technique, you absolutely must pay the card's balance in full each month.

PART II

Choose the Best Sites

CHAPTER 3

Choose Your Ceremony Site

You want to choose a ceremony site that's beautiful and meaningful to you, but did you know that you can save money by choosing certain sites over others? Did you know that you can waste money by not checking out some ceremony sites fully for their restrictions, thereby causing you to lose money when you have to cancel musicians and other details because they're not allowed at that location? Read on to learn more about the types of sites and the types of issues that can affect your bottom line.

13. Considering Different Types of Sites

First make a date with your fiancé to sit down and talk about where to have your ceremony. Set aside a few hours and together list some of the possible places for a wedding. Perhaps there are some you haven't thought of, and this time together can inspire you to consider them as potential candidates for the perfect wedding site.

Try not to rule anything out at first. Sometimes a location that's not a church or synagogue that seems expensive at certain times of the year—especially a destination wedding location—may be affordable during the off-season. There may be upgrades and amenities available if you persist in thoroughly investigating a promising location. Maybe the setting sounds good to one of you but not the other. At least do some research, consider the possibility, talk about it, then decide.

The ceremony site will dictate everything else about the wedding—attire, reception possibilities, transportation requirements, decorations—so it makes sense to start planning the wedding here.

Some couples want to have both the wedding and the reception in the same place. They don't want a big gap in their day, especially if time spent taking photographs after the wedding will slow the celebration down. Then again, the location may simply lend itself to having both ceremony and reception there, since it has the perfect party room, the perfect décor, and would prevent you from needing to hire limousines to get from one place to the other. An all-in-one location might be just what you need to save money.

If, however, you want to be married in a religious ceremony in a church, synagogue, or other place of worship, it's fine to have the reception elsewhere. Sometimes a church or synagogue doesn't have a reception hall or can't accommodate your needs.

By this point in your life, you've probably attended several weddings and observed (even critiqued) even more on television and at the movies. You've formed an idea of what's important to you. Regardless of whether you have a modest or a luxurious budget, it's very important to incorporate your priorities. If you have your heart set on a seaside location, don't rule it out because you live in a landlocked area. Rethink your options and be creative. If you can't travel to the water, maybe a gorgeous park with a fountain will work just as well.

Locations for ceremony sites are almost limitless. Picture your wedding in each location you and your fiancé consider; then make appointments to visit your final choices. The only way to fully investigate a site for its beauty and functionality is an in-person tour. Consider the time you spend going there to be a great investment in your day.

Planning a Religious Wedding

Many couples choose to have a traditional ceremony in a place of worship. Sometimes they're an active member or frequent attendee, and they can't think of any place more appropriate. Other couples, who don't necessarily consider themselves religious, still want to be married in a religious setting. Perhaps such a site is traditional in your family, and you find yourself looking for a place of religious significance for your wedding day.

Keep in mind as you tour houses of worship that some require you to be an established member of their congregation. They might not allow you to marry there if you are not on their list. Or, they might charge you an exorbitant price if you are a nonmember who wishes to marry there. It sounds awful, but some couples have a very difficult time booking a religious site for their wedding when they run into red tape this way. They sometimes find themselves looking at different houses of worship, perhaps outside their faith, to bring a religious element into their day without being limited by too many regulations.

Speaking of regulations, some houses of worship have lengthy lists of what they don't allow. Some don't allow any secular music, so there goes the guitarist you wanted to play the music for your ceremony. Some don't allow photographers, since the flashes can damage their artwork or icons, so there goes the photographer you wanted to book. Some have strict rules about having you cover your arms or your shoulders or your head, which could limit the dress you have in mind. It's important to ask the house of worship's clerk for a printed list of their rules before you hand over your deposit payment, to be sure you won't be prevented from including some of your most wished-for wedding elements.

Ask too about their schedules for religious holidays. Some churches, for instance, won't perform weddings during Lent.

Many houses of worship will also require you to participate in pre-wedding counseling, sometimes at expense, to fulfill their requirements for marrying you. Do you want to do this? Do you have time? Do you live close enough to the church to fulfill this requirement? Would they accept a letter of completion if you take the course in a church near where you live? There are a lot of details to cover, so ask plenty of questions and take plenty of notes before you book any religious site for your wedding day. It would be a horrible surprise for you to find these things out later.

Planning a Non-Religious Wedding

A wedding ceremony can be just as spiritual in a nontraditional setting. Once you start looking at alternative places for your ceremony, you may find that the savings over a formal church or synagogue wedding can be significant in some cases. Some sites do not charge the fees charged by houses of worship, and they may not impose so many rules on you. But some sites do charge site fees you need to be aware of. Every establishment has its own rules, and you need to be aware of them and adhere to them so that your next planning steps do not turn into wasted time and money.

Consider Country Clubs

Country clubs may be ideal for weddings. Ceremonies can take place outdoors on or near a golf course or indoors in the clubhouse. Receptions can also be held on-site, and you can rent golf carts as convenient transportation for you and your guests. Country clubs with spas often offer special pampering packages for the bride and her attendants, often at reduced rates as a thank-you for booking the wedding there. Sometimes the bride's spa services are free. Some country clubs require that you be a member to be married on their premises, but this is not always essential. Perhaps a relative or guest can be a member, and you be married there based on their belonging, and this membership can net you a discount on the wedding package prices.

Private Clubs

Look into private clubhouses that are owned by neighborhood associations in upscale residential developments. Cities have waterfront civic buildings that can be ideal. Check the Yellow Pages and newspaper bridal sections for locations that can provide a country club atmosphere for much less money. You'll find private clubs for women's associations, men's clubs, and any number of special interest groups such as the Junior League or other group to which a friend or relative may belong.

Historic Homes

Historic mansions or plantations can be elegant sites; they are often so beautifully furnished and landscaped that they require little decoration for the ceremony. Such a location lends itself to photogenic backdrops for your wedding album. Check out stately historical homes in your area, which you can find through your local historical society or chamber of commerce, even your local tourism department (*www.towd.com*). Through these resources, you might find a historic inn, lighthouse, or pier that would make a unique setting for your wedding. These historic sites can often be rented for a small donation, sometimes just a hundred dollars, and by virtue of being a unique location with so much visual attraction, it can look to your guests as if you spent a lot more money than you did.

Museums and Cultural Centers

Museums and cultural centers make lovely sites for weddings with their displays of artwork and elegant settings. Again, by virtue of being a unique setting with eye-catching décor (that you don't have to pay for!), your guests will think you've spent a fortune to hold your wedding at this site, instead of knowing how much you saved. Just be sure to inquire about the type of artwork that will be on display at a museum, since you don't want to marry while surrounded by any graphic or violent images that could offend your guests.

Casual Settings

Casual wedding sites include parks, country farms, even country and western clubs where you, your new spouse, and your guests can do the two-step after the ceremony. Your local tourism department is going to be a terrific resource to show you the availability of unique settings, as well as inform you about all reservation requirements, permits, and limitations. Some parks, for instance, are only open until eight o'clock in the evening, and you might not be allowed to bring in any musicians or cook food there for the reception.

BRIDAL BONUS Look online at *www.celebrantsusa .org* to find potential officiants to interview and check out their price packages, and ask your other wedding vendors whom they have seen work in the past and would recommend. Individuals other than ministers or rabbis can officiate at your wedding. Your county courthouse has information on how to become an officiant for a specific date or event. Even if you don't save money over the cost of hiring a member of the clergy, the honor of having a friend or family member marry you is priceless.

Alumni Settings

Some couples meet while attending college, and so getting married in the college chapel or outdoors in a special spot where they met or studied together can be memorable. More and more couples are finding that getting married there feels "just right," and is the fitting transition to a new life together. Is there some special place that has meaning for you and your fiancé? Why not make it a part of your wedding day? Keep an eye out for ceremony sites that can double as reception sites, for extra savings.

Explore Additional Sites

Marinas are growing in popularity, since many couples love the big picture windows overlooking the beautiful yachts moored right outside, as well as the marina's dockside terraces and open-air settings for a great indoor-and-outdoor ceremony setting. You can get a great view of the sunset to perfect your ceremony as well. Again, membership has its privileges, including lower prices, so ask if any of your contacts belong to a yacht club or marina club. Another top option is a restaurant located right on the beach, overlooking the ocean. You can hold your ceremony on the beach, accompanied by the sound of the pounding waves, and then go inside the restaurant for the reception.

Visit prospective locations together. If you find a location you like, stay there for a while to see whether you feel the kind of mood you want for your wedding. Factor in noise level, likely temperatures, and acoustics.

14. Think about Seasons and Timing

When it comes to your wedding ceremony, the season of the wedding might offer you an added perk: the site might already be decorated for a religious holiday, such as filled with Easter lilies or lined with colorful poinsettias for Christmastime. This means the existing décor becomes your wedding décor, and you don't have to spend a fortune on altar floral arrangements, pew décor, or any other expensive accenting. Ask the site manager to explain what their usual décor is for the different religious holidays, since some holy times mean that the church or synagogue is stripped of all décor out of reverence for the holiday.

The same applies to non-religious settings. For a winter wedding, will the ballroom already be decorated with twenty-foot evergreen trees decorated with pretty ribbons and bows? Will the hotel lobby be decorated, the perfect setting for your post-wedding photos? Will the setting be decorated with potted pink tulips for spring? When you ask in advance, you may find out that the site already has a lavish and expensive décor plan that all of their brides and grooms get to enjoy. Couples who are not in the know waste a lot of money by ordering floral décor, which they sometimes can't even use!

If you'll be at an outdoor site, ask about the trees and plants that will be in bloom at the time of your wedding. Ask to see the site's collection of wedding photo albums, which most sites keep to show their prospective bridal clientele. There, you'll see the tulip beds, the lilies, the little red flowers lining all the paths, the cherry blossom trees in bloom, the weeping willow tree providing the perfect "altar" for your vows . . . and you won't even have to hire your florist to make an arch for you! It's already there.

Speaking of already there, you may be able to find out if there is another wedding taking place at your location on the same day. It might be a longshot, but perhaps that other bride and groom would like to speak with you about using the same décor for both weddings, and splitting the bill between you. That gives you 50 percent off your ceremony site décor expenses.

You won't be able to contact the other couple. The site will let them know of your interest, and they'll put you in touch, if indeed you do have similar tastes for decorating the site. And don't forget that you can use the early-morning bride's decorations as the basis of your own, with permission from her, of course. This means having your florist go into the ceremony site and add colored ribbons to her all-white pew décor, add some candles to the aisle, place just two small altar arrangements on either side of her one big white one. This can save you plenty of money, if the site will allow you to do so.

15. Take It Outside

Outdoor locations are all around you, from state and local parks to arboretums to vineyards and family farms. There are beautiful parks located in nearly every community, many with pavilions, gazebos, or other special structures that make for a truly lovely ceremony and add a natural dimension to your wedding that usually means—again—that you don't need to spend a fortune decorating a blank-slate ballroom. For you, the trees in bloom, the colors of the leaves, even the blue sky above provide all the atmosphere you'll need.

If you live near the ocean, you can get married on the beach at daybreak or sunset. There's nothing quite like standing near a vast, serene blue sea for a backdrop to a new life together.

Outdoor locations can be less expensive than a church or synagogue setting, but often present some extra legwork and challenges. For instance, you will need a permit to have a wedding or public gathering in many parks, and arboretums are private property that will require you to book your wedding on their grounds for a fee. Some botanical gardens, in some pricier regions of the country, can charge exorbitant site fees, since they know the beauty of their floral wonderland is a big draw for weddings. If you're on a budget, you might not even want to consider these big-name gardens for your big day.

Site fees and permits aside, an outdoor setting will require you to have shelter in case of bad weather. This often means renting a tent that suits the size and style of your wedding. Ask plenty of questions before you arrange for tent rental, since some sites will not allow tents to be staked into their grounds! They don't want their lawn ruined, so they forbid tents. That would be awful to discover after you already paid for yours! The best plan is to choose a location that offers both outdoor areas for your ceremony and an indoor ballroom where the ceremony and reception can be located in case of inclement weather. You don't need to spend extra . . . you just need your site staff to relocate all of those chairs inside.

Speaking of chairs, be aware that many outdoor sites will require you to rent a lot of items. From chairs to tables to linens and everything else on a wedding supply list, the expenses can run very high. So be sure to factor in the prices of rentals when you're looking at any outdoor or unique site that doesn't have its own tables, chairs, and serving items on hand. This can be a dealbreaker when you find a site with no site fee, but it would cost you thousands of dollars just to have enough wineglasses!

Outdoor settings also require restroom facilities, which you may have to rent. You'll find a range of portable styles from the types you see at construction sites (not appropriate for a wedding!) to luxury motor coaches with marble bathrooms and an attendant who hands out warm towels to guests. This essential expense can take a chunk out of your budget, so think about the need for a restroom before you fall in love with, and book, any outdoor site.

Every ceremony site presents its challenges, no matter where you are, so just be prepared to get the permits or extra rental items you need to make this site a reality, and find ways to save in other areas of your wedding plans. Remember, the ceremony site is actually the centerpiece of your big day—it's where you take your vows, and where you marry. So spend plenty of time researching everything that is involved in booking the site of your dreams.

16. Think about a Private-Home Wedding

Private homes, which have long been used for weddings, are becoming more popular with couples who want a smaller, more intimate wedding with fewer guests. Whether your home is large or small, a wedding held there can make you and your partner feel comfortable and cherished. It also adds to the very special history of a home, where you may have climbed your first tree, where you played kickball in the yard, where you celebrated your childhood birthdays. Many couples say an at-home wedding provides the perfect backdrop for celebrating the next big chapter in their lives. "I dreamed of walking down our staircase to meet my husband-to-be from the first time I saw my family home as a little girl," a friend once confided. "I used to practice walking down the steps, holding a feather duster and pretending it was my bouquet. My mom and dad were thrilled when I asked if my fiancé and I could be married there. We stood before the fireplace and exchanged vows."

Which areas of the home are perfect for a wedding? Most families arrange to set up a tent in the backyard, or have an open-air wedding situated around their yard, garden, terrace, or pool area. The money they've put into sprucing up their home is now an investment in the wedding décor, with that rose trellis providing floral color, the outdoor furniture serving as a buffet area, the new deck as the perfect place to take family photos. Money your family has already spent has created the ideal wedding setting.

As for indoor areas, you might establish that the first floor, the living room, dining room, and den are the only areas open for guests' milling about. You can tie a garland across the stairwell so that no one gets into the bedrooms upstairs, and that garland wrapped around the banister also becomes part of the décor.

Fireplaces add to ambiance. Family photos on the walls are pre-existing décor. Families also love to show off their kitchen remodel or their new sundeck. The perks are everywhere.

Where are the budget challenges? Rentals. That tent is going to cost a bit, as are extra tables, buffet tables, chairs, china and crystal patterns, and a serving staff to hand out appetizers and serve as bartenders. When your wedding takes place outside an established ballroom or restaurant, you have to think like an establishment owner and provide all of the help you'll need.

A wedding coordinator is priceless in this regard, letting you know exactly how many bartenders and servers you'll need.

> **WATCH OUT** Don't try to save money by hiring fewer servers, bartenders, and valet parkers than your coordinator suggests. You don't want long lines at the bar, cars left in the street, or servers not able to move through your crowd before their platters are picked clean. Hire as many people as you are advised, even if it costs a bit more. Your guests' experience is very important for the success of the wedding.

Be sure to get extra home insurance for your at-home wedding, so that you are protected in case any one gets injured on your property, and ask your town hall about permits you'll need to host a big event at your home. You may be surprised to find you need parking permits, or that there's a noise ordinance in your neighborhood that means the band has to shut down at ten o'clock in the evening, or else you get a $5,000 fine.

At Home, Somewhere Else

Perhaps a friend or family member has a house with a lovely garden patio or a pool where a reception could be held. Be considerate if one of your loved ones agrees to host your reception. Preparations and cleanup for the big day can be disruptive, so make sure the host is truly willing to make this sacrifice. Be sure to let them know exactly what will be involved, when the setup crew needs access to the home, when the florist needs to come see the house, when the caterer needs to pre-screen the kitchen to be sure the oven is big enough. Those who are generous in letting you use their homes should be treated with the utmost consideration. And have their home professionally cleaned after the party.

Be prepared for the added expense of some things going wrong, such as a vase being broken by a dancing guest, or some mud tracks on the carpet. A big party in a private home always means that some unexpected marks will happen, and be sure to put all valuables away in locked safes since you will have some strangers on your property setting up the décor. Guests' dates may wander through the home too, and you don't want anything damaged or missing.

17. Plan a Destination Wedding

For some couples, there's nothing better than a destination wedding, which can provide the opportunity to gather friends and family before the wedding for a festive time. Even with the expenses of airfare and hotel room reservations, bringing just twenty or so relatives and friends along for a getaway wedding can save the couple a large amount of money. They don't, after all, have to pay for everyone's travel and lodging unless they want to. They won't have a guest list of three hundred people to feed. They may even have a smaller bridal party, or none at all. They choose to keep it simple, and take advantage of resorts that offer amazing getaway wedding packages. Some resorts offer free photography when you book with them. Some offer free drinks for all. Some offer a free honeymoon when you book your destination wedding with them. The trend is so big, and so attractive to wedding couples on a budget, that you'll find many different packages out there that can turn your wedding budget into the perfect way to get a much more elaborate wedding ceremony and celebration than you could have had back home.

A destination wedding can be held anywhere in the world, including on any of the oceans, in big-city locations, at ski resorts, in overseas locales, even a few states away from your home, perhaps in your favorite tourist area. Cruise ships offer wedding packages, and you can choose any number of exotic locations in the world for a wedding. But you don't need to get carried away. A nice beach ceremony a few states away could satisfy you.

WATCH OUT There can be a number of challenges to planning a destination wedding. You might have to deal with unfamiliar regulations, work with vendors you don't know, and have fewer guests at the wedding. This final point can be seen as either a negative or a positive, depending on how you feel about having certain family members at your wedding! All joking aside, destination weddings require significant planning.

Find a Great Location

Again, wedding coordinators can help you locate the perfect getaway locale, and many planners will travel with you to take care of the plans! You can also visit *www.destinationbride.com* to read the reviews of a wedding coordinator who specializes in destination weddings and can point out terrific deals, warn you about questions to ask, just making the process easier on you.

Many resort chains such as the Hilton or Westin have properties all over the world, and their websites connect you right to the destination wedding planning team that they have on staff. This team will, usually for free, instruct you on the rules and regulations of getting your marriage license in order, and help you connect with their favored vendors and planners to give your wedding ceremony a local flair. Putting a destination wedding together has become such a well-planned method in so many places that you'll often find that all of your plans come together with just a few phone calls or e-mails with their team. You usually will not have to travel to the site unless you want to; the coordinators take care of everything, and are always willing to answer your questions.

As for other locations, Disney World in Orlando, Florida, offers a variety of wedding services in their many themed hotels, with the bonus of fun and adventurous honeymoon options right there in the theme parks. It's a stateside destination location that may also appeal to your guests, particularly if children will be attending.

Riverboats that traverse the Mississippi or a river near you are also hot spots for weddings. Couples can choose to reserve an entire cruise or just a portion of it. A special plus: The captain can perform the ceremony.

> **BRIDAL BONUS** Most tourism offices have coupon books for their locations, and in them you'll find free or discounted passes to area restaurants, tourist attractions, sporting events, movie theaters, and countless other attractions. These coupon packets can save you hundreds of dollars, and if you tell your destination wedding guests about them, they too can call or write to get their own packets of savings to use during your wedding weekend.

Look for deals online by typing your requirements into a search engine such as Yahoo! or Google. Try simple phrases such as "wedding packages under $500." One couple found a Lake Tahoe location that offers several packages starting with a simple economy wedding for $275, which includes obtaining, filing, and notarizing the marriage license. Upgrading with more elaborate flowers, more chapel time, videography, and additional features increases the price, of course. The most expensive package tops out at several thousand dollars and includes a three-hour stretch limousine rental.

Bed-and-breakfasts, inns, vineyards, and similar settings offer opportunities for elegant wedding ceremonies at varying prices. Some vineyards specialize in wine-pairing meals; others can provide lodging for you and your guests. Check out the prices for these types of sites in your desired location, again going to the tourism office directory at *www.towd.com* to get connected with an office and experts who can lead you to the best deals possible.

The best part of a destination wedding is using the location's natural elements—the beautiful natural setting of Hawaii, for instance, inspires a special mood for a wedding ceremony. Perhaps that is why it was one of the first destination wedding/honeymoon locations, and to this day remains a premier site. What is it about your potential destination site that inspires you to say your vows there? The scenery could mean you won't have to spend a dime on décor. The relaxed setting could mean you're well-outfitted in a sundress or a bikini and sarong instead of a $5,000 wedding gown. And here's the best part: If you book your destination wedding at an all-inclusive resort, everyone eats and drinks for one modest price. This could save you thousands of dollars and is one of the biggest selling points for destination weddings today.

CHAPTER 4

Find Your Perfect Reception Site

A great reception site has to be more than just a pretty room. The setting for your celebration is connected to the number-one wedding expense: the catering. So choosing the best location for your reception often goes hand in hand with arranging for your guests to be well fed while they're in an attractive location. There are a lot of issues to address, a lot of research to be done, as you look for the perfect location for your big party, so let's get started with the most important steps to get you where you want to be.

18. Research Sites Well

Your first step is collecting information on a range of reception sites that are known for being in a moderate price range. Your recently married friends are the ideal resource, since they previously explored the price packages at many reception halls and booked the best ones. You'll get insider stories on which packages were the best, and which sales managers were the nicest, and most generous with discounts and free additions to packages!

Your wedding coordinator and other wedding vendors will also be happy to recommend the best, and best-priced reception sites in town, and you'll often get the most honest appraisals from experts like the photographer and videographer who work everywhere in town and are fed at the receptions.

Visit at least two places that each of you thinks would make a good reception location. The idea is to stay flexible in your thinking, and to brainstorm. Sometimes the planning for a wedding becomes so intense that you just want to make quick decisions, pay the money, and settle matters. Getting it settled, however, should not mean settling! So don't rush through this most important part of your wedding plans. It's just too important to the success of your wedding, and the safety of your wedding budget.

Some reception sites have their own caterers, but other sites require you to find your own. Some places will let you bring in your own caterer, but will charge a fee for not using their services. You may prefer the convenience of an all-in-one package over the responsibility of locating a reliable caterer. Be sure you get information for a variety of scenarios as you do your research.

The answers to questions about food can significantly affect your decision, and certainly affect your budget. Be mindful of time, money, and energy—and of your priorities—as you make your decision.

19. Look at Traditional Ballrooms

Holding your wedding in a traditional ballroom delivers big savings in the form of not having to rent tables, chairs, forks, spoons, because they're already included when you book the site. You'll also have access to the site's chefs, servers, bartenders, and valet parkers without having to hire workers from an independent company. Within the all-inclusive reality of a ballroom wedding are the price-specific packages you'll be given when you inquire about the site for your wedding day. You should know that most ballrooms do not post their wedding packages and price lists online, so you will have to contact the sales team at the particular banquet hall or hotel where the ballroom is located. Most often, they'll e-mail or snail mail you a packet of detailed price packages for receptions, as well as catering lists for the rehearsal dinner and morning-after breakfast (if the ballroom is located in the hotel where guests will be staying). You will often find that hotel special event sales managers are only too happy to reward you for booking your wedding there by giving you big discounts on the other special events for your wedding weekend, such as the rehearsal dinner. Some couples get up to 40 percent off their rehearsal dinner packages just for booking the wedding at a ballroom that checks out okay upon inspection.

The key is to take the time to research ballrooms well, since you'll find different perks in different places. For instance, a hotel might host just one wedding per weekend day, or it might host up to five or six different weddings, which you can hear through the very thin divider doors, turning a giant ballroom into six smaller ones. With multiple events going on during the same evening, as you may find at the least expensive ballroom in town, you might find that the service is sloppy, the food lukewarm, party crashers are drinking at your bar, and any number of other dilemmas caused by your not having the run of the grounds. So cheaper is not always better.

Speaking of grounds, a terrific ballroom might be situated on a property that also has lovely gardens for phototaking, a terrace for a cocktail party, fountains, a great view. Always be sure to take a walking tour of the grounds before you sign on the dotted line.

Another benefit to traditional ballroom weddings? The staff has plenty of experience with planning weddings and seeing them to fruition, they may have worked with your vendors before, and their servers know exactly how to work the room. With a team of experienced servers and captains, this site often means guests may be served with professionalism, and that often includes a ballroom's ability to whip up that unexpected kosher or gluten-free meal because its proximity to the hotel kitchen means lots of additional foods are in stock.

And again, if the ceremony and reception are held in the same place, notably this hotel ballroom, no one has to spend money on transportation, and only one site needs to be decorated. This location could potentially save you thousands of dollars, and still give you the effect of a very expensive traditional wedding.

20. Look at Church Reception Halls

Perhaps you both like the idea of having the reception in the hall attached to your church or synagogue. Nearly one out of four couples who marry in a church have their reception in the church hall, often because the bride or the groom, or both, are members of the church and it makes sense to stay there after the ceremony. There's a sense of rightness to the place that makes you want to continue your celebration there.

There's no question that it's very convenient to have the reception at your place of worship following the ceremony. Guests can move easily into adjoining reception space while you have your wedding pictures taken, and you don't have to worry about your guests navigating busy highways. Weather is another factor. For instance, if you're having a winter wedding in a cold climate, staying inside in one location is a bonus.

WATCH OUT Check with the church regarding its rules about using the hall, particularly about any restrictions on serving alcoholic drinks and dancing. It may also have rules about hours for hall rental and how you may decorate the place.

Because you already have an established relationship with the facility, you have a reduced risk of complications, conflicts, and potential crises. That's not to say you shouldn't be just as diligent about setting expectations and getting the details in writing, but you can find some peace of mind in knowing that you're familiar with your venue. You might also be granted a waiver of the church's usual site fees, since you are a recognized member of the congregation. If your family has donated money to the establishment, you might be treated to a gold standard of services, including such add-ons as free use of church musicians for the ceremony and reception.

Caterers say they enjoy working in many church halls because the kitchens in their reception halls are large, spacious, and situated close to the seating areas where guests await their food. Since the site is used for group events, you might even find that the church or synagogue features a catering-sized refrigerator in which large trays fit, as well as a deluxe oven and plenty of counter space. It's quite common for a church hall to be a better fit for a caterer than someone's private home with a narrower refrigerator and less counter or prep space.

BRIDAL BONUS As an added savings, members of the church community often volunteer to "work" weddings, sometimes preparing all the food as a group, for far less than catering prices. They may also decorate, handle setup and cleanup, and serve as a master of ceremonies, announcing your first dances and other important parts of your reception.

Convenience and price breaks are fine reasons to remain at your church or synagogue. Add to that the fact that most reception halls are well maintained and often decorated, and you have quite a plus.

21. Look at Alternative Sites

In the previous chapter, you read about various alternative sites for your ceremony—including alumni clubs, country clubs, marinas, museums and bed and breakfasts—and these sites are also quite magical for wedding receptions. For any alternative site that is not well practiced in large social events (as a hotel banquet hall staff would be), you'll need to spell out your wishes and expectations, and often hire additional workers such as bartenders for a B&B that does not have a set bar but is the perfect locale for your by-the-beach wedding celebration. When you speak to these sites' managers, ask about their rules for servers, especially if there is an agency with which they like to work. Many locations like museums and B&Bs are often the sites of special events, including charity events, so the owner is well acquainted with a great staffing or special events company. And perhaps the site has an in-place 30 percent–off coupon for wedding couples!

Talk to your wedding vendors about their favorite alternative reception locations, and gather a list of places to tour. This is one area where a wedding coordinator can be invaluable, leading you to the perfect winery or private estate home that can be rented out while the owners are vacationing in Switzerland. An in-the-know events expert knows all of the best sites in town, and also the important questions to ask for each one, such as if the planned renovations will be completed by your wedding date, or if the nearby airport's flight path has been changed recently. You don't want your wedding buzzed by landing Gulfstreams, right?

Some alternative sites such as alumni clubs will often hire undergraduates or graduate students as their staff and servers at a price that's on the budget side, so be sure to ask what the staff will be wearing as they work your wedding. You are within your rights to ask them to wear black pants and white shirts to look a little more formal, as befitting your day. Since these are students who will be working your wedding, be generous and tip them well at the end of the event.

An unexpected alternative site is the party room at your favorite restaurant, perhaps the restaurant where you got engaged! These smaller banquet rooms might hold only sixty people, so there is your perfect reasoning for limiting your guest list! "We really wanted to hold the wedding at this particular restaurant where we got engaged, and their party room has a fire code that only allows sixty guests, so we had to cut the guest list down. Sorry!" gets you out of inviting those extra hundred distant relatives and your parents' coworkers! Sometimes the site you fall in love with can help you with the larger, foundational aspects of your wedding plans.

22. Consider an At-Home Reception

The most important element of an at-home reception is making sure your caterer—or whoever is preparing the food you'll serve —has everything he or she needs to prepare the food properly, store it, refrigerate it, heat it up, and serve it. That can call for a lot of rentals, including a separate tent just for the caterer's use (as might sometimes be a requirement). If you do not have an oversized oven or refrigerator to suit the caterer's oversized trays, you might need to rent additional heating and cooling units so that all foods are kept safe from spoilage and served at the right temperatures.

Again, a tent, tables, chairs, and table settings will be needed for all of the guests, and you can cut down on this particular expense by borrowing sets of china and crystal from friends or relatives, and mix-and-matching to create a different look at each guest table. When you keep your guest list on the small side—again, using space as a deciding factor so that you can avoid guest expectations for the sake of limited space—you may be able to use your own china and crystal, or just a few sets from your parents, sister, and friends without paying hundreds for rented sets.

Many at-home receptions take place in a living room that has been cleared of furniture. The couches and reclining chairs have been moved upstairs to a separate storage room, and the living room becomes a stylish mingling room or dance floor for no extra rental charges.

Your fireplace at home provides ambiance, and you might even set your home entertainment center to play a DVD of videos of the two of you, or concert footage DVDs of your favorite artists, as if they had been hired to play your wedding . . . only for far less.

An at-home wedding might require a higher rental list, but you can use many of your own items, such as linen tablecloths for the cake table, candelabras, vases, centerpiece blooms cut from your own backyard flowering trees.

Schedule the rental company to come pick up your chairs and other supplies on the morning after the wedding, often for no extra charge, and have a cleaning service return your home to spotless that day or the next day. A professional cleaning service team may come with a discount if you find them through your wedding coordinator who often helps clients prep their homes for at-home events . . . he or she might have a contact at the cleaning company who has arranged for clients to enjoy 40 percent off their usual rates . . . and those drapes will get vacuumed for the first time in a long time as well!

23. Take Advantage of Seasonal Pricing

Even if you're not looking at traditional wedding sites, such as hotel ballrooms or banquet halls, for your reception site, be aware that alternative sites also stick to the price hikes and cuts of their in-season and out-of-season times of the year. While you may know that the hotel in town charges through the roof for an October wedding, you might find that a nearby bed and breakfast has slashed its rates in half because fall foliage season is over, and they're trying to attract some extra business.

When the school season starts up again, museums might be busy with charitable events to raise funds for private schools and universities, so you might find that they are in-season during September with their prices almost doubled for site fees and services. Winter months might be a better time for them, with January prices often 60 percent less than the fall.

Understand supply and demand, and don't be afraid to ask the site manager to tell you exactly when their busy season is, and when they're looking to book more events. You might even find out that the location has openings in less than three months, and they're practically giving away the wedding date booking at a 70 percent discount per guest! If that works with the rest of your plans, this research might get you to book your wedding date for two months from now . . . worth it as it is to have a big, formal wedding that you would never have been able to afford without that gigantic discount. Many couples book the open date, and keep their guest list the same size, so that they save a few thousand dollars and essentially honeymoon for free.

BRIDAL BONUS Check *www.festivals.com* to find out when and where arts, music, and cultural festivals will be taking place in your area. You might want to avoid a busy time in town, or you might see the festival as a great way to provide your guests with lots to do—on their own dime—during their visit for the wedding.

Ask the site what the season holds for them. Will they also be hosting a professional association's corporate retreat at the same time? Will they be home to a cultural conference? Is the town planning a big festival at the time of your wedding?

24. Work with In-House Vendors and Their Rules

Some sites require you to work only with their in-house caterer or their in-house florist. The site has a contract to work solely with that person, and as such you won't get the benefit of comparison-shopping among a group of different caterers or florists. This is a big danger to a wedding budget, since comparison shopping is a key way to find the best-priced and best-quality experts in town. When you're told by a site, "you will work with our guy," you will not have the freedom to find a better deal elsewhere. You're stuck, and that can cost you.

So be careful before you sign with a location. Be sure you know their rules about whether or not you can hire vendors from outside their walls. It could be a matter of thousands of dollars on the line.

If you do have the freedom to hire outside vendors, the site might give you a list of their Approved Vendors. You can work with anyone on this list, but no one off the list. This allows you some comparison room, but it still limits you. You may be able to find a great vendor with the perfect price package from these contenders, so it might not be a problem. Just ask lots of questions, and use the money-saving tips in this book when you interview or work with any vendors you hire.

Your site might also suggest a longer list of recommended vendors, which provides you with a great starting point for investing the time it takes to call and meet with each of the interesting ones, ask plenty of questions, and find out how each vendor conducts weddings of your style and in your price range.

Next, find out which limitations the site imposes. If they do not have any power sources outside, then your deejay would have to run a power line many, many yards out to where the tent will be set up. Does the site have adequate parking for your guests? A safe trail on which guests can walk to the reception clearing? Is there a noise curfew because the site is located in a residential area, meaning your party gets shut down at nine o'clock in the evening?

You have to request the site's printed list of limitations so that you know what you're up against, and what you might not be able to book for your wedding day.

PART III

Planning the Celebration

CHAPTER 5

Plan for Smart Catering

*R*eception food is usually calculated on a per-person basis. For instance, let's say you want to invite 200 people for a sit-down dinner, and the least expensive individual meal you can get at your reception site is $30. Simple math quickly shows this will cost you $6,000. But what if you don't want to spend that much on reception food? You have two options: You can either keep the number of guests to a minimum, such as paying for only one hundred guests to attend and eat, or you can work a little budget-saving magic through the decisions you make on the catering itself. In this section, you'll learn how to cut your catering costs without sacrificing taste, because the food is one of the most important and most memorable parts of the wedding celebration. It is possible to save lots of money in this area; you just need to go about it in the right way.

25. Think about Sit-Down Dinners

Traditionally, the sit-down dinner consisted of three to five courses—sometimes seven courses for ultraformal or tasting menus—and often cost in the higher end of most couple's budgets, just because of the sheer volume of food with so many courses. Wedding couples who want to stick with tradition in their family but worry about the price do not have to skip the sit-down meal! You can have the sit-down dinner, just with a few twists to narrow the volume of food. First, eliminate a few courses, such as the appetizer course and the soup course, particularly if you will be having a cocktail party before the sit-down dinner. It's just repetitive to have another appetizer formally served to seated guests, so you can ask the caterer to eliminate that course from your order. Guests can start with salad, then get a small pasta dish, their entrée, and look forward to dessert!

You'll also find in-the-menu budget-cutting concepts later in this chapter, which you can use while working with your caterer to devise the menu for your sit-down dinner.

Here's a little tip about sit-down dinners that might cost you less. Ask the site manager for Vendors' Meals, which may be chicken and veggies rather than the salmon your other guests are getting, which might cost you just $15 or under per vendor. Ask also if kids eat for free! Many reception halls now feed the little ones under age ten for nothing, and kids between ages eleven to sixteen eat for half the adult price! If you have multiple vendors, hire a band, or have lots of kids coming to the wedding, this one question is going to save you hundreds of dollars.

> **WATCH OUT** Many wedding guests complain that there was too much food at the wedding! How is this possible when the point is to impress them? As with all things, there's a fine line where it turns into overkill. If you'll have a large cocktail party, scale down the dinner. Guests prefer to be served a smaller amount of delicious food than be bombarded with endless courses of so-so food.

Another money-saving factor is the style in which the food is served. Did you know that hand-passed food items often cost less because guests eat fewer of them than if they were set on a buffet table? Caterers say that hand-passed (where a server carries a silver tray of food to the guests at a cocktail party) costs you 20 to 40 percent less.

If you'll set up a buffet for your dinner party, fill the buffet with two-thirds budget dishes and one-third pricier meat dishes to keep costs down. When you fill a buffet with lots of lush, fresh salads, turning meats and seafoods into centerpieces of those salads, you can provide a beautiful dinner buffet without spending a fortune. With a buffet, guests can serve themselves, and you won't have to pay for extra wait staff. Letting guests select what they like also keeps wasted food to a minimum (some adults still won't eat vegetables!).

Dinner Stations

Dinner stations are becoming increasingly popular at weddings, and not just at cocktail parties (which we'll get to in a minute). Now, the sit-down dinner or buffet dinner features elegant and themed stations in an array of tastes and budget levels. Make it a rule: when you choose a unique way to serve any type of dish, and it's something your guests don't get to eat every day, it looks as if you spent a lot more on your menu. Guests want to enjoy terrific foods at a wedding, not suffer through the same dry chicken they get at corporate luncheons. So look at the upcoming tips in this chapter for ways to turn your food choices into something very special.

And don't forget that you have several different parts of a dinner meal where you can make an impression. Think about stations or buffet platters with lots of fresh or steamed vegetables, grilled eggplant, and other non-meat specialties that guests don't often cook for themselves. And again, those salads are always crowd-pleasers.

As a delightful and inexpensive food station for any buffet or sit-down dinner, ask your caterer to arrange the bread, rolls, and breadsticks—along with butter, olive oil, and tapenades—in special stations for guests to help themselves. Especially if you ask for the bread—which is often included in most catering menus—to be served warm, with soft butter, you give the effect of a gourmet meal. And it could be free.

26. Plan a Classic Cocktail Party

When you choose a cocktail party reception, it's not always an automatic savings over a sit-down dinner. You could, after all, choose very expensive foods for your cocktail party and end up paying more. The key to turning a cocktail party into a savings is in the individual menu items you choose, and—here's your money-saving formula—serving your pricier items hand-passed by servers, not at buffet tables or at food stations where you need to supply more food to guests who will automatically eat more pieces per person.

One great way to save is to select a theme for your cocktail party reception. For instance, if you choose a fiesta theme, you can save a lot of money by arranging for fajita stations where each beef, pork, or chicken fajita needs only a few strips of meat and is then dressed up with lots of fresh vegetables and toppings such as salsa.

If you want a Far East theme, caterers say you can save a fortune by serving lo meins in which less meat is needed, and the flavor comes from terrific egg noodles, vegetables, and sauces.

Forget about having a carving station with a prime rib, pork loin, ham, or other big slab of meat. Guests would rather enjoy smaller pieces of meat incorporated into a salad or marinated and grilled strips.

Forget about having a raw bar with clams, oysters, and other pricey seafood. As a savings of over 70 percent, you can accent pasta dishes with a sprinkling of cooked crab, some shrimp, or cooked lobster meat that makes an impression on guests.

Take advantage of comfort foods, such as little dishes of mac 'n cheese, mini hot dogs wrapped in dough, mini meatballs, and other party favorites that guests love. Caterers say these treats, even at formal weddings, are just as crowd-pleasing as dishes you might look at to try to impress your guests. Most would rather have pigs-in-a-blanket than caviar on toast tips any day, and you save thousands on your cocktail party menu.

27. Bet on Brunch

A suggestion for a simple breakfast or brunch menu in the modest budget category could consist of scrambled eggs, bacon or sausage, potatoes, fruit, sweet rolls, coffee, tea, and juice. This general menu can be adapted for a moderate budget. Offer omelets with several fillings, two breakfast meats, home fries or grits, an assortment of breakfast pastries, coffee, tea, hot chocolate, and several juices.

A luxurious wedding breakfast or brunch includes eggs Benedict or a similar egg specialty, crêpes or Belgian waffles, spiral-sliced ham or shrimp cocktail, fruit compote, flavored coffees or cappuccino, teas, several juice selections, and mimosas (champagne and orange juice cocktails). Or plan an elegant lunch of a chicken or fish dish with a few elegantly prepared vegetable dishes. These menus will cost less than the meat menus often served at dinner receptions. Chicken can range from simple, inexpensive dishes up to coq au vin. Seafood can be broiled with a light sauce for a modest or moderate budget; luxurious budgets can splurge on lobster. Your caterer can make suggestions based on your budget.

BRIDAL BONUS Some couples are skipping wedding meals by scheduling their reception at nonmeal times, such as in the midafternoon or after dinner. Featuring a selection of hors d'oeuvres or a dessert buffet with appropriate beverages at these off-meal times is a very classy option and can save you 40 to 60 percent off your budget. One popular trend right now is the dessert and champagne reception, where guests are treated to a buffet of chocolate mousses, wedding cake, pies, fruit tarts, and dessert crepes as that something different that guests think means you spent more money on, but you really haven't. A dessert reception might cost just $20 per guest, including champagne, wine, or coffee.

Keep in mind that hotels often offer their own brunch buffets for a fraction of what dinner catering would cost elsewhere, so you may be able to book a private room with that same buffet served only to your guests. You get the carving stations, the salads, the omelettes, and even free champagne and coffee in some instances! At one New York City wedding, the couple found a Sunday brunch buffet for just $30 per person, a savings of over $120 per guest from the dinner catering prices they found elsewhere. Their private-room brunch was elegant, guests loved the upscale breakfast foods and full desert buffet, and they could hear the hotel's harpist from inside their reception room . . . for free entertainment.

28. Handle the Off-Site Caterer Issue

If you are having your reception at a hotel or a restaurant, you will have to use their catering services. One of your reasons for choosing that location is presumably because you want to serve their food, and their catering packages were priced well. You have left all of the food preparation and storage up to the experts at your site. But what happens if your reception is at a location that does not have food service? You will either have to prepare the food yourself, or hire an off-site caterer. Many couples who don't want to spend the days prior to their wedding preparing food, or who don't want their relatives cooking on the wedding day, decide to research, interview, and hire an independent or off-site caterer to become the chef at their chosen wedding location.

The most important factor is hiring the right caterer. Get a list of potential caterers from your reception site or from other vendors, such as your wedding coordinator or florist. See whether there's a culinary school or an educational institution in your area that provides catering services; you'll save money and also help students launch their careers. For a smaller wedding of under fifty guests, a personal chef may be able to create the food for your event. Look online at your regional wedding websites to gather names of candidates, interview well, and go for tastings to see if you like a particular caterer's work. Food can sound great on a printed menu list, but it's how the food tastes that determines if you've spent your money well.

Do tell the caterer that you're on a budget, and that you're looking to his or her expertise for ways to create a fabulous menu for less. Every chef has secrets on how to stretch a dollar and turn a regular chicken dish into something unforgettable.

29. Design Twists on Cheaper Foods

Regardless of who provides the food, you can save money by asking a lot of questions and carefully looking over menus so that you receive the most for your budgeted dollars. If either the on-site or the private caterers tend to feature very gourmet entrées, ask whether you can substitute something less expensive.

Being careful with your dollars doesn't mean serving an institutional chicken dinner. True, chicken and pasta have long been known as the least expensive dishes in catering, but a great caterer can take a cheaper chicken breast and turn it into an unexpected gourmet masterpiece. Think creatively: Certain herbs, spices, and other fairly simple touches can transform a bird into something quite elegant and less expensive than coq au vin.

One secret of superstar caterers who create amazing meals on low budgets is to use a fabulous sauce, such as a spicy mandarin orange sauce for chicken dishes, or a mushroom and garlic sauce for pork, a Madeira sauce for beef medallions. A terrific sauce allows you to dress up inexpensive beef, chicken, and pasta dishes, at less than you'd pay for filet mignon and salmon.

Even if you want to splurge and have prime rib, not all guests eat beef these days, so you want to provide something different for them anyway. Caterers say it's a smart savings to provide a non-meat entrée for your guests who are vegetarian and for those who just want something lighter. Since guests know they're going to eat a lot at the cocktail party, they often love a vegetable-based meal. Thinking outside the box with your entrée choices can mean a delicious meal for less money.

You could also save by allowing the chef to substitute different seafood and fruit (with your approval) if he hears of a better price or better in-season quality. Especially with seafood, prices vary by market availability. Lobster might cost three times as much if there are weather problems along the food supply chain. If you tell your caterer to call you a week before the wedding to let you know about discounts on other types of seafood, including shellfish, you could save thousands just by switching to a tilapia entrée rather than salmon.

30. Include Pricier Foods, but Smartly

You can include shrimp, clams, oysters, and filet mignon in your wedding menu, and at significant savings when you choose the right style of serving them. Here are the best ways to incorporate pricier foods into your menu and still save hundreds on your catering bill:

- Serve food hand-passed. Have your caterer design a hand-passed hors d'oeuvre based on the pricey dish, such as shrimp cocktail or beef skewers with dipping sauce, which will provide just a few bites to guests during the cocktail party. By contrast, if you put shrimp on the buffet table, some guests would load their plates and make it a meal, eating ten people's worth of food.
- Use it as garnish. A dab of caviar on a potato pancake provides upscale flair and taste for way less than if you set out a tin of beluga. The same goes for seafood, served cooked and diced on top of pasta or meat dishes.
- Make it a side dish. Instead of serving lobster tails to everyone, turn lobster meat into a side dish when mixed with green beans or risotto.

- Use it as crêpe filling. Seafood crepes are popular entrées and cocktail party station dishes, so include pricey lobster and other seafood chunks in creamy seafood-crepe fillings for less.

- Create combination platters. Rather than give guests their choice of prime rib or salmon – which would require your caterer to buy enough food for every guest to change his or her mind, thereby doubling the shopping order – design a combination platter that includes a few grilled shrimp or a smaller square of salmon, a few medallions of beef, and lots of vegetables and risotto for a full platter of delicious food at a lower price than the expected salmon dinner.

31. Choose DIY Menu Items

You're not really going to have that reception without Aunt Anna's special antipasto platter, are you? Or Grandma Joanna's special-occasion champagne punch? Or your best friend Nancy's incredible cake?

Family inclusion has always been an extremely important part of wedding days. Perhaps some members of your family would like to get more involved in your wedding, and food preparation is a perfect opportunity. You won't know unless you ask. If you ask friends or family members and they seem reluctant, don't push the issue or make them feel guilty. But if they truly want to help, great. This will add such a personal touch to your wedding. Do you have family favorites? Even if you have a caterer prepare your food, there may still be some foods and beverages you just can't imagine being fixed by someone other than a particular family member or friend.

BRIDAL BONUS DIY doesn't always mean that you or anyone else has to slave away over a hot stove to prepare an appetizer, platter, or dessert. You can very well bring platters from discount warehouse stores such as Costco or Sam's Club, where even seafood can be found for less, party sandwich platters cost 20 percent less than at many delicatessens, and dessert platters rival those you might otherwise order from your own baker. Think about what you or your team of volunteers might be able to find at Costco, at great savings. Take your team to your local store to scout out the catering options and perhaps even get a taste of their frozen hors d'oeuvres heated up and served in mini cups on the weekends. You may find even more savings than you expected on food items you never knew could come from a discount warehouse store.

Check to make sure you can bring those special food and beverage items to your reception site so they're not wasted or feelings aren't hurt. There should be enough of whatever is brought for every one of your guests to have a taste, and the food or beverage should be stored at the proper temperature so there is no food-poisoning issue to ruin the day. Make sure that your cooking volunteers are made aware of just how many appetizers they will have to make, and what you would like done to keep them cool during the trip out to your wedding site, where they'll need to be heated up, and what is needed to plate these dishes in an attractive manner. Perhaps other friends and family have platters you can borrow for these homemade dishes to fit in with catered options.

The most popular DIY catering dishes are less labor-intensive, such as a big batch of chili that can be spooned into small cups or bowls as an appetizer. A relative might have no problem whipping up a big platter of their signature veggie and cheese lasagna for guests to dig into. Slow cooker recipes such as pulled pork are also crowd-pleasers, and they're easy to heat up in a microwave if necessary.

CHAPTER 6

Designing Low-Cost Drinks

*W*hat beverages will you serve at your reception? Time of day plays an important part in determining your best options. Bottles of champagne or other alcoholic beverages aren't freely passed around at a morning wedding reception. A mimosa or maybe a Bloody Mary could be offered at a brunch, but there would be a limit on the number served because of the hour. At luncheons and mid-afternoon weddings, champagne punch or a glass or two of champagne is appropriate. Again, the time of day dictates that the amount be controlled. During late afternoon or evening weddings, there is no need to control the amount of alcoholic beverages. Rather than serving champagne, some couples choose to serve one drink that reflects the theme of their wedding, like a Mojito for an island wedding.

Alcohol can be a huge expense at a reception. Do you want to have a champagne toast? Do you prefer top-shelf liquors—the best brands available—or would mid-shelf be fine enough for your crowd? How long is your reception? You'll need to make sure your site has acquired enough liquor to suit your guest list.

> **WATCH OUT** You'll need to check on the alcohol policy at your reception site. Some church reception halls, fraternal halls, and community centers don't permit alcohol at all; many hotels and restaurants want you to buy from them. Before you purchase cases of liquor, be sure you're not wasting your money. It would be a shame to find out later that you can't serve any of what you've bought. Ask also if the site charges a corkage fee, which is a set amount of money for each bottle of wine opened. You may be able to negotiate that fee out of your contract, or limit the number of bottles that may be opened. Specify as well how many bartenders you will need. Don't attempt to save money by having too few. The more, the better. It's worth the expense.

32. Cheer for Champagne

If you would like champagne served at your wedding, you can arrange for this upscale drink for less money. Rather than stock enough champagne to serve guests all throughout the reception, arrange for each guests to be poured a half-flute of champagne, just enough for one champagne toast. The bubbly doesn't have to flow freely with a magnum at each table. Just a taste of the good stuff is fine.

Research and taste-test champagne if your site allows you to. You might find a great vintage of champagne that you wish to serve for less. Visit *www.winespectator.com* for reviews and awards on the newest vintages of champagne ranked by price, and ask wine shop owners for their recommendations.

Skip the champagne and let guests toast you with the drinks they have already chosen for themselves, such as wine, beer, mixed drinks, or colas. What matter most are the wishes they send to you as they lift their glasses.

33. Set a Limited Bar Menu

Rather than have a full open bar where guests can get any type of liquor they want, for any type of mixed drink possible—which would require your site to stock hundreds of dollars worth of liquors and charge it to you—choose just a few different types of mixed drinks such as gin and tonics, classic martinis, Jack and Cokes, plus several different vintages of wines and several different types of beers. You'll save a lot of money when your bartenders only need certain amounts of liquors from a set collection of bottles you've purchased through them.

Choose great moderately priced wines that you have found through *www.winespectator.com*. You'll be surprised to find how many great wines there are under $20 per bottle. When you taste-test them, you may find they're perfect for your wedding, and perfect for your wallet. If you're not a wine expert, get a friend or a helpful person at the wine shop to guide you in selecting a good vintage with a reasonable price.

Eliminate drinks that require a large amount of alcohol per serving, such as a Long Island Iced Tea, and refuse to serve shots of liquor to guests. This keeps your usage lower and cuts down on expenses.

The same rules apply if you'll be setting up your own bar for your at-home wedding weekend parties, or for the reception itself. Find a terrific discount liquor store and talk to the staff members there to get recommendations on the best-priced and tastiest drinks. They can steer you away from the most expensive types of rums to a different, less expensive brand that tastes wonderful.

34. Set a Limited Bar Time

Arrange with the site manager for your bar to be open for a shorter period of time, perhaps closing it down an hour before the reception ends. With service ended early, you could save 20 to 40 percent off your liquor bill. Coffee may be served for the final hour of your event, which will save you a fortune in liquor expenses. If you like the idea of closing the bar early but don't want your guests to miss out on having a drink or two at the end of the evening, you can arrange for the bartenders to put a bottle of wine or pitcher of sangria on each guest table for self-service.

> **BRIDAL BONUS** If you will close your bar early, make sure you let guests know so that they can get their final drink of the evening. Print on the guest table menu cards, "The bar will close at 5:00 PM for the dessert hour. Coffee will be served at that time."

35. Serve Nonalcoholic Drinks

Some families do not believe in having alcohol at weddings and family events, and some couples simply like the idea of limiting alcohol consumption at the wedding—both look to the idea of having plenty of nonalcoholic drinks as a way to save lots of money. Here are the top ways to supply a variety of nonalcoholic drinks for your wedding:

- Set out different types of punches on different tables or bartops.
- Create a nonalcoholic sangria, which is essentially a fruit-laden punch served in a pitcher on each guest table.

- Provide several different flavors of iced teas, including green tea, raspberry tea, white tea, and more, for a refreshing drink at a summer or outdoor wedding.

- Add slices of fruit to pitchers of ice water to create a colorful effect on guest tables or drink bars.

- Shop at discount warehouse stores like Costco and Sam's Club to get cases of soda for less money.

- Ask if the site serves soft drinks for free; if it's not their policy, ask if you can be granted free soda at your event.

- Don't buy cases of name-brand bottled water for your wedding. Tap water is often fine, especially when served with lemon or lime slices.

- Serve nonalcoholic versions of mixed drinks, such as a virgin daiquiri just for the icy treat and colorful drinks in everyone's hands. Especially on a hot day or at an outdoor or beach wedding, these drinks are a nice treat without the dehydrating factor of alcohol.

CHAPTER 7

Select Your Wedding Cake

How much do you want to budget for your cake? If you have a modest or moderate budget and the cake is not one of the most important elements of your day, you can save a lot by making the right decisions on your cake design.

When deciding on a cake, first consider your needs. How many guests are you inviting? Do you want to save the top layer of your cake to freeze and enjoy on your first anniversary? Will you want a groom's cake as well? Your baker needs to know the answers to these questions in order to tell you how big a cake to order. The size and complexity of the cake, as well as where and when it needs to be delivered, will determine the price.

36. Choose a Simpler Design

A five-tier, intricate wedding cake can cost over $1,000 in some areas of the country. While the wedding cake is an important focal point at the reception, there are ways to design a pretty cake that's delicious to eat. Remember, it's not just about how the cake looks! Design something simple like a two- or three-layer cake iced simply and topped with flowers, which is often the least expensive choice of cake design.

Ask for cake layers to be set right on top of each other, instead of separated by columns or elevated in any manner. A simpler style of design and easier transport will save you money.

Resourceful ways to save on your wedding cake include using fake layers to add height but not dollars; in this design, only one layer is a real cake, and the other layers are circles of Styrofoam iced with matching frosting. You cut the real layer of cake in your cake-cutting ceremony, and then it's wheeled into the kitchen where a separate, inexpensive sheet cake has been cut and plated for each of your guests.

Since it's the detail that increases the price of a wedding cake, just order a simply frosted cake with minimal piping or frosting rosettes, which takes the baker less time to create. When you ask for intricate icing, a copy of the design of the lace from your dress, or sugar-paste flowers or marzipan birds on your cake, that's when prices skyrocket. Always choose design elements that are easier to create to keep your costs down. And don't forget that you can decorate a professionally made cake, by adding your own florist-approved fresh flowers, a circle of ribbon around the base of each layer, or your own piped icing designs. See page 103 for more on DIY cake options.

> **BRIDAL BONUS** There are so many choices—think of them as opportunities to save! You'll save your money by going with bakers you've found through references from family and friends. You can find a traditional wedding-cake baker or ask your caterer to bake you a cake. You can order your cake from a grocery store bakery or have a friend or family member make it. If you'd like a simpler style of cake, such as a plain-white frosted round cake that you'll decorate yourself, check prices at Costco.

Specifying your order in writing ensures that the cake you pay for is the same one that is delivered to your wedding. Don't order a bigger cake than you need. If you're serving desserts or having a groom's cake, you won't need as many slices. Remember, not everyone who attends necessarily wants a slice of cake.

37. Decide on Low-Cost Flavors and Fillings

First decide what flavor of cake you'd like. If you find that you like a white cake but your fiancé prefers chocolate, you can serve both—it's your cake! Simply ask the baker to do different layers in different flavors. In most cases, this will not be an extra charge, but you should ask to make sure. If your baker does charge extra for alternative cake types per layer, negotiate that charge out of your bill or decide on one cake type.

Also, keep in mind that gourmet cakes such as carrot cake or cheesecake usually cost extra, sometimes double the price of traditional cake, so those flavors might be better for your own homemade confection for the rehearsal dinner or for the groom's cake. Speaking of groom's cakes, if you're on a budget, you can skip this tradition. Most sites offer a gorgeous wedding cake (which might be included in your reception package!) and additional desserts, so you may not need this extra cake.

The most important factor is looking at a baker's list of fillings and cake flavors and choosing your favorites from the standard-priced list. Many bakers offer a range of vanilla, chocolate, mocha, and other basic flavors for their one basic price, but they will charge more for more gourmet flavors and filling, such as fruit mousse or fillings made with liqueurs like Amaretto and Grand Marnier. In some regions of the country, you may find cannoli or espresso buttercream fillings at nearly twice the price of standard fillings. Of course you want your cake to taste great, but that can be achieved with a moist, delicious cake and the perfect regular buttercream filling.

Buttercream is a standard filling and can be made in just about any flavor from vanilla to chocolate to strawberry, lemon, and more. Some bakers charge extra to add real strawberries to a buttercream filling, since that's an extra step in the preparations. Not to mention the seasonal and market price of strawberries. When couples want a bit of texture in their cake filling, they can get that crunch by asking their baker to add mini chocolate chips or mini mint chips, even mini peanut butter chips to the buttercream filling mixing bowl, rather than pricier nuts or shredded coconut.

Ask about price differences between buttercream and whipped cream frostings. Most bakers will not charge more for one or the other, but it's a question you should ask in case they do.

> **WATCH OUT** Believe it or not, some bakers will charge extra for colors of frosting that are outside their usual pinks and greens for flowers. Before you request any special colors for your cake, ask to make sure there isn't an added fee.

Fondant, a mixture of sugar and water cooked to a consistency that can be rolled and molded over a cake, has become very popular because it helps keep a cake fresh and elegant despite the weather. Fondant too is usually more expensive than frosting, due to the extra labor involved in creation of the fondant, rolling it out, and placing and cutting it to size. Some people do not like the taste of fondant, so perhaps this is an added expense you can skip.

38. Choose a Cake Topper

Once all wedding cakes had to have a bride and groom on the top. Only a few other types of toppers were deemed acceptable. Today it seems like anything goes. Couples are encouraged to try something different and express their imagination. A cake can be decorated with icing patterns that look like lace or fresh flowers and be placed on an antique porcelain cake stand.

Personalize your cake with something that reflects your interests, such as your career, hobbies, or your military experience. Do the two of you like to skydive or scuba dive? You might want a cake topper to show off this interest. Individuals who make custom cake toppers can make something special that may become a treasured family heirloom. Given a picture or detailed description of a specialty cake, local bakers might be able to duplicate what you have in mind for a lower price.

Another way to save is to use an heirloom cake topper, such as the one your parents used on their wedding cake.

Or skip the cake topper completely and just have your florist place a tuft of fresh flowers on the top layer of your cake, with cascading blooms or individual flowers decorating the lower layers. This natural look is quite inexpensive, often possible for under $20.

39. Look for Cake Alternatives

One clever bride chose to serve lovely flower-trimmed cupcakes arranged on a tall, tiered pedestal stand. That way each guest could have an individualized serving, which saved on the price of a big cake. The children at the wedding weren't the only ones who were delighted. The cupcakes were very moist because they were baked in paper wrappings, and the icing details were as decorative as that on a full-sized cake.

Small versions of wedding cakes became a trend several years ago and were very popular with wedding bakers because they could charge more for the extra work of creating them. While the little cakes are lovely, you'll have to think about whether you want to budget the amount of money you'll pay for them.

Ask your baker if you can arrange for one small cake just for décor, and then provide an array of inexpensive baked items such as petit fours or pastries for guests to enjoy. You can also get these baked items at your local grocery store or Costco for just a fraction of what bakers charge. And don't forget that chocolate-dipped strawberries are an elegant, inexpensive secondary dessert to accompany the wedding cake.

These days, budget wedding couples are skipping the endless Viennese table covered with pies, tortes, cakes, mousses and other desserts, because it turns out to be just too much food for guests who are already full on the terrific food you served at the cocktail party and the dinner. You simply don't need that many desserts, especially when you look at what reception halls charge for such a spread. In some regions of the country, it can be an additional $20 to $40 dollars per guest. In a catering package, you may be able to order platters of petits fours for just $5 dollars per guest. Do some negotiating, and ask what you can arrange for a lower-priced dessert offering.

Skip the dessert stations that require an attendant to whip up Bananas Foster and other liquor-based desserts, since these are often quite pricey.

Some low-priced dessert alternatives include ice cream bars, where guests can make their own sundaes. Also popular as a gourmet twist: gelato or chocolate mousse bars. And you can add some healthy treats with a big fresh fruit platter that you have arranged to be removed from the cocktail party spread and served instead during the dessert hour, for free.

Make Your Own Cake

Don't shy away from letting a friend or family member make your cake. Perhaps one of them has taken a cake decorating class or you've seen her produce wonderful cakes for special occasions. She would most likely welcome the chance to bake your cake as a wedding gift.

Craft stores carry supplies to make wedding and other special-event cakes. There you'll find cake pans, plates, columns, frosting decorations, and toppers—everything you need for a wedding cake.

> **BRIDAL BONUS** You can now find fondant at craft stores. Once available only to professional bakers, fondant is a creamy sugar paste that can be used decoratively in place of traditional frosting. There are even special rolling pins for rolling out the fondant before placing it atop the cake. Bakers will tell you that fondant covers a multitude of sins, transforming an ordinary cake into a beautiful work of art. Cracks disappear beneath it; crumbs don't show through as they often do with frosting. Fondant also keeps a cake fresher longer. Amateur bakers can now produce a professional-looking cake.

Make Your Own Desserts for Less

You can also save a fortune by making your own desserts, or allowing friends and family to make their own signature desserts to bring to your reception (just ask for the site's permission first!). Crowd-pleasing dessert may include brownies, blondies, chocolate mousse served in martini glasses that you get for free from the site, or rent for just a dollar per glass, chocolate chip cookies, macadamia nut cookies, frosted cookies designed to work with your wedding color scheme, nut bread squares, and even store-bought cookie platters from the discount warehouse store that provide a range of tasty treats for half the price of caterer-made desserts. Visit *www.foodtv.com* to find great new dessert recipes to try ahead of time, or dig into your family recipe collection to see if you can duplicate a relative's masterpiece fudge bars.

Bring a touch of seasonal flavor to your DIY desserts, such as those macadamia nut cookies for an island-themed wedding, or sugar cookies frosted in holiday designs for a winter wedding. Many couples on a budget plan a dessert-making party with their helpful volunteers, a pleasant evening at their home where everyone bakes and frosts together, creating a budget spread of desserts and some fun and stress-free conversation with loved ones. It gives you desserts made with love, and without high prices.

PART IV

Choosing Your

Wedding Wardrobe

CHAPTER 8

Select Your Wedding Dress for Less

*E*very bride dreams of the beautiful wedding dress, and the start of the planning process often involves Internet searches to see the newest designs and designer offerings. In that dream-come-true visit to the bridal gown shop, accompanied by your excited bridesmaids and mom, the fairy tale of the designer gown hits a brick wall when you get your first look at the astounding pricetags. $5,000 for a dress you're going to wear once? This is, after all, a very important dress, and the wedding industry knows that excited brides can sometimes agree to pay anything for the gown they want. But you don't have to take the bait and agree to pay an exorbitant amount for your dress. There are plenty of ways to get your dream gown for less. The secrets are here in these tips.

40. Establish Your Style

What budget have you set for your dress? Remember that you do not have to be bound by a smaller budget for your dress if it is one of your "priority" items for the wedding. Perhaps you want to spend more to get what you want and cut down on expenses elsewhere. This is perfectly understandable. It's an important day for you and you want to look gorgeous. After all, you'll be looking at those wedding pictures for a long, long time.

Keep your ceremony and reception locations in mind. A big, formal dress with a sweeping train won't work if you have to walk down a grassy path outdoors for your ceremony—well, not unless you don't mind grass stains or are willing to spend the dollars to rent a runner! A dress with long sleeves for a summertime outdoor wedding won't work either. Grooms are nervous enough. They don't need to see you fainting right in front of them!

Do you want a long gown or a short one? Simple or elaborate? You can find a gown for any kind of budget, depending on your willingness to compromise. Want an elaborate gown for a little money? You'll find your source in sections to come. Start your gown search by looking through bridal magazines and websites. Clip pictures of the dresses and styles you like. Also, look through any photos you can find of weddings that have taken place in the location you've chosen. Countless bridal websites will help you decide on the dress style you prefer, so you'll know what you want when you're ready to go shopping. Doing your homework first is useful if you aren't well versed in bridal-couture jargon.

Know the Terminology

Knowing the types of necklines and other features and whether they look good on you will also save you time and money in the bridal stores. When you speak the same language, you and the bridal consultant can work together to find what you want. You also won't be as likely to let yourself get talked into something that isn't you or that's out of your price range.

Know your silhouettes before you shop:

- A-line gowns are shaped like the letter A, with fitted bodices and flared skirts.
- Ballroom gowns are characteristic wedding gowns, with full, billowy skirts.
- Empire-waist gowns have a waist that starts under the bust and a slim skirt.
- Mermaid gowns are fitted dresses with a flare on the bottom of the skirt.
- Sheath gowns are form-\fitting dresses.

BRIDAL BONUS The sooner you start looking for your dress, the better. If you wait until the last minute, you're going to feel desperate and spend too much. You're also taking a chance on not finding what you want at all. Your wedding day is not the time to feel as though you could be wearing something better. Start looking for a dress six to nine months before the wedding. This ensures that you have enough time to find a dress you love and have it altered in time for the wedding.

Look Beyond White

Color is a hot trend in wedding dresses. At the bridal salon or at any other shop, look beyond the white or off-white gown to a dress that has some color in it. Some wedding gowns may be pale pink, or have colored embroidery in the bodice. A new trend from the fashion runways is to wear a metallic gown as something different. If this is your second wedding, you might not want a white dress, so you are apt to find savings in these nontraditional, and thus not so in-demand, dresses in the shop's collection. Colored gowns might be priced 10 percent less.

And don't forget that you can buy an inexpensive simple white dress and add some color of your own, such as adding a colorful sash to a white dress from a formalwear store. Put some sparkle on a simple inexpensive dress with a fabulous pin or necklace. Your creativity can turn a $100 gown into a stunner comparative to those pricey designer gowns for less.

Don't forget that an informal wedding could mean that you'll wear a sundress or halter dress bought at a department store for under $100 as well. Add a bridal bouquet, and it's the perfect look.

41. Know Where to Shop

The savings might be right in the bridal salon where all of those expensive dresses are shown. Look through the shop's racks of discontinued or last season's dresses. Remember that just because a manufacturer has decided to go in a different direction this season doesn't mean that last season's designs are now unfashionable. Years ago, after wedding dresses with huge, puffy sleeves were discontinued, there were plenty of brides delighted to look through the previous year's designs on the bargain rack. You may find savings of up to 80 percent off on gowns that are considered dated, but they look just fine to you . . . or you could take a dress bought on sale and make some decorative changes to it.

Ask at your bridal shop whether they carry sample gowns at reduced prices. You might be lucky enough to get the gown you want at a discount. There may also be slightly damaged dresses that can be quickly and easily repaired. Or, dresses that have been purchased by other brides and returned to the shop for a partial or full refund. The shop owner might agree to sell you that gown at a discount to avoid the expense of returning it to their supplier.

Bridal gown shops have lots of lower-priced dresses to select from. Just tell the shop owner or sales clerk what your actual budget is, and he or she will pull selections for you to make the process easier and save you time.

Visit Consignment Shops

Consignment shops are good places to find bargains. Sometimes brides buy a gown and then change their wedding date, and the gown is no longer appropriate for the new season. There you have it—a never-worn gown at reduced price!

Go Vintage

Although vintage shop gowns can be pricey, you can still find bargains. Especially consider this option if you are getting married in a historical setting, such as in an old local mansion. A vintage dress will complement the ambiance of the ceremony site and make you feel elegant. Gowns from the 1920s and 1930s have inspired the slinky styles fashionable today and often don't cost much. Finish the look with vintage accessories like a long string of pearls or glass beads, a beaded purse, or a period hat.

Vintage clothing is a marvelous touch for weddings of all budgets, depending on the quality and age of the garments.

One caution, though—larger sizes are harder to find in vintage clothing. There may also be special cleaning or alterations that will drive up the cost.

Hit the Bridal Outlet Stores

Bridal outlets are springing up in more and more cities these days. Even if you don't choose a dress bargain advertised for $99, you will find a large selection of dresses. Be careful of pressure to buy, both in the huge warehouses and in smaller specialty shops where overhead is high. If you have a year to plan your wedding, it's possible to shop at the end of a season for the new season the following year.

Drop into Department Stores

Most importantly, be creative. Keep your mind open to different solutions. Check out department stores, especially the formalwear sections, and catalogs. That simple, floor-length cocktail sheath could be a perfect wedding dress; all you need to do is add a few decorative touches. Visit the prom dress or debutante section of formalwear stores to find perfect and stylish dresses (many of them in white!) for under $100. It's one of the best ways to find a wedding gown bargain. Many of these dresses look just like wedding dresses and cost far less. Remember to search department stores when the stores have their big sales going on. You might find the perfect formal dress and get an extra 20 percent off.

Cruise the Classifieds

It's possible to find a lovely dress and stay within budget through newspaper classified ads, where brides who changed their wedding plans will often advertise their gowns for sale at a fraction of retail price, and often throw in the veil for free. Some bridal gown shops will also unload their outdated collections by advertising sales or individual dresses in the classifieds, which you can access for free through newspapers' websites.

> **BRIDAL BONUS** One bride found a beautiful gown by visiting local dry cleaners, where brides have been known sometimes to abandon their dresses.

Check Out Sample Sales

Sample sales are a smart way to buy a designer gown at a discount price. Bridal salons sell their sample gowns once the manufacturer discontinues them, usually a seasonal occurrence. Bridal salons take great care to keep their samples in good condition, but usually they will have been tried on by a number of customers. Slight imperfections are unavoidable, but you can replace a zipper, have the sample dress professionally cleaned, and still come out ahead. Sign on to the mailing lists for bridal shops, and you may receive advance VIP notice of an upcoming sample sale where you'll find dresses and accessories on sale for up to 70 percent off. Your favorite bridal gown designer's website will often list the schedule of their upcoming sample sales or trunk sales, and you'll be able to search for when the tour comes to your hometown. Sign on to attend, and you may be able to get your gown for a huge discount. It could be the find of a lifetime. Just be sure you're going to trunk sales, and not trunk shows, since trunk shows feature the designer's current dress line at lower or no discount.

42. Consider Heirloom Dresses

For a priceless (in both senses of the word) opportunity, look in your mother's closet. For sentimental reasons many brides wear the gowns their mothers, grandmothers, or other female relatives wore. Especially in the past few decades, your relatives may have had their gowns professionally preserved, so that hermetically sealed box will deliver a dress that's fresh and non-yellowed, a discovered treasure that saves you a fortune and can mean a lot to your family.

If a family gown is still in good shape, you can have it professionally cleaned and altered. Some brides use portions of an heirloom dress, such as keeping the bodice and skirt, but removing the sleeves and the train. Occasionally, the more delicate headpieces don't survive storage but can be easily replicated by either you or a seamstress with the aid of wedding photos.

43. Borrow a Dress

Do you have a friend or relative who will loan you a dress? Nothing's better than free—well, free except for what you pay to have it cleaned before you return it!

Consider sharing a gown. Two sisters shared a gown for their weddings that took place a few months apart. They loved the idea because they'd always been very close emotionally and this made for a special bond. Because of the cost savings, they were able to spend a little more for better quality. Fortunately the two were close enough in size that the second sister needed to do only minor alterations.

In the news recently, a group of ten brides-to-be group-purchased a designer wedding gown, and they took turns wearing it to each of their weddings over the course of two years. Since every bride is beautiful, and since these women put their own design elements to work on the dress—such as adding sleeves or tying a colored sash at the waist—no one ever knew this was the same dress. Could your circle of friends agree to such a plan? Perhaps just three or four of you would be interested in finding a very basic design of dress and then dressing it up to suit your design styles? With this plan, you might pay only $500 to $700 for that $5,000 designer gown, or just $50 to $70 when you buy that dress in a consignment shop or online. Imagine that! Paying 1 percent of the retail price!

Think about Dress Rentals

Renting a dress is also an option. Think of it as leasing your dream dress and not paying all that money for one use. One bride who was having a luxurious wedding decided to save money by renting her dress. "No one knew," she said afterward. "Since the rest of the wedding was so nice, it wasn't as if anyone suspected. We were able to spend the money on having a nicer reception." Check online for dress rental companies, including tux shops that often branch out into renting formalwear for women as well. Most rental companies shop at designer trunk sales, nabbing that Vera Wang at 70 percent off, and then they turn a profit by renting that dress for under $300 a pop, usually only to five brides maximum to avoid wear and tear. This could be your secret to getting your dream designer gown for a small amount of money, and if your heart isn't set on keeping and preserving the dress, you just return it after the wedding. Some rental agencies will rent dresses for a flat fee of $75 or $99, which makes this source a great budget find.

44. Investigate Online Sources

Today, many brides are finding their dream gowns on eBay and other online auction sites. eBay is full of wedding-gown styles at bargain prices offered by individuals as well as bridal stores. You can find tiaras under $15, gowns for $25, even a $4,000

Vera Wang worn just once for $1,500. When you do a search of bridal gowns, you'll see just about every designer name possible, along with detailed pictures of what the seller has to offer. Remember, many bridal gown shops need to unload last season's dresses, and this is where they are going to sell their old stock at huge discounts. You could wind up finding a pricey designer dress for well inside your budget range.

Some creative brides find gowns listed for just $50 apiece, and they buy several with plans to use the train from one dress, the sleeves from another, and the bodice from another. For just $150, they have now acquired designer dress elements to construct a gown they saw in a gown shop for several thousand dollars.

> **WATCH OUT** Whether you use eBay or a lesser-known auction site, it's important to be a smart consumer. Be honest with yourself about sizes and preferences. Don't buy a dress that will need lots of alterations, such as a size 14 when you are a size 4, because that will eat away at whatever you've saved by purchasing your dress at auction. Also, buy from reputable and well-rated sellers and protect your investment by secure transactions.

You will also find online gown stores where you could order a dress right over the Internet. While prices may be attractive, you have to be very careful about online fraud. Always buy from a reputable dealer. Instead of a website you've never heard of, look at the websites for store like Ann

Taylor (*www.anntaylor.com*), where you'll find their special occasion dresses for prices often under $200 and sometimes on sale for under $50! You may also get free shipping if the store is offering a special. Department store websites also show formal dresses and bridal collections for sale prices. If you're nervous about ordering online, just use these resources as a way to find out where the nearest Ann Taylor or department store is, so that you can go there and try on the gowns that are on sale. Your bridesmaids can join you, too, to help you choose your gown and perhaps find their own on-sale dresses as well.

Online research is done by over 95 percent of brides, who most often go shopping in the stores they find listed on websites. They don't want to miss out on the special treatment and in-store experience of shopping for a wedding dress! Buying books online is one thing . . . a wedding gown is another!

45. Order a Custom-Made Gown

You can have your gown custom-made, using a picture you've found in a magazine, online, or in a dress pattern at the craft store. If you don't feel comfortable sewing an entire wedding gown by yourself, enlist the help of a professional seamstress to make a dress to your specifications. A custom-made gown sounds expensive, but it is often less expensive than brand-new dresses from bridal salons, and you will get exactly what you want.

Your seamstress can work with you to design a dress that is uniquely you, but it helps both of you if you have an idea of what you want even before your first meeting. Bring pictures of wedding gowns you admire and be specific about what you want. The more detail you can express, the better.

Find a seamstress through your network of friends and associates. Meet with her to discuss your vision. It's important that you feel a connection and are able to communicate with your seamstress so as to avoid any misunderstanding later on. If you don't feel the seamstress shares your vision for your dress, look elsewhere. Finally, ask for and check references.

Do you favor a simple design yet love the beadwork on a more expensive gown? Consider buying the beads from a fabric store and either having your seamstress expertly apply them or sewing them on yourself to save money.

Some enterprising brides go to nearby fashion academies to find students who would love to be commissioned to make a wedding gown. You have to have a lot of trust and allow for a lot of time for fittings, but these talented undiscovered superstars can create one-of-a-kind masterpieces for a fraction of the cost. You will provide the fabric, found at a fabric wholesale store or craft store, and the student will work with you to create the look you want. Afterward, that student gets to use photos of your gown as part of his or her portfolio. Some brides report that their students only charged a few hundred dollars for hours of work. Never ask a student to work only for the sample in a portfolio; that's insulting. Find fashion academies through an online search, and check at nearby universities for referrals to their fashion departments where instructors can recommend their top students.

46. Save Elsewhere

If you'd like the designer gown, and you've fallen in love with one at a salon, at retail price, you can still have it! Just adjust your budget to allow for the higher amount in this top priority item, and find ways to save in other areas of your budget. You might, for instance, forgo new designer shoes and wear silver heels you already own. You might eliminate new jewelry and wear the necklace your mom wore on her wedding day. There are always ways to beat the budget, so that you can get these extra-special elements for your day.

47. Save on Alterations

Find a dress shop that offers free alterations when you buy your gown from them. Some shops will recommend well-priced seamstresses with years of experience—and remember that a good alterations job is essential for your gown to fit your body perfectly. So you should never try to take on this job yourself, since that's a disaster for a wedding-day look, especially when seams split or hems fall. While some relatives will offer to do the alterations on your dress, it's often a better decision to go with a pro.

CHAPTER 9

Save on Accessories

You've found the perfect gown, and now it's time to add those beautiful bridal accessories to perfect your look. When you look in bridal shops, you'll see pretty shoes, veils, and more, but they are often priced high because they're capturing you while you're in wedding mode, often willing to spend more in the excitement of shopping for your gown. Look for alternative sources and choices to get these pretty pieces for less.

48. Save on Shoes

For your special day, you may want new shoes. But don't think you have to go for those pricey white satin ones you find in the bridal stores and on wedding websites. Begin your search at discount stores, and look in the regular shoe section of any footwear or department store for shoes that complement your gown. If you like, dress them up with clip-on shoe jewelry available at these stores. Whatever type of shoes you choose, try to buy some that you can wear after the wedding.

Make sure you pick out a pair of shoes you find comfortable, since you're going to be on your feet a lot on your wedding day. The same is true for your attendants: Don't force your bridesmaids to hobble down the aisle in shoes they might not feel at ease in. Check out the shoes you want to wear for comfort. There are many adorable styles that have low or flat heels, which are especially necessary for outdoor weddings!

Speaking of comfort, there's often no better way to ensure a good fit than to wear shoes you already own. More brides are opting to wear their own plain white heels for the wedding, wisely remembering that the shoes are not in the spotlight for the majority of the wedding day. They're covered by the dress, and only on display at certain times of the event. Another money-saving trend is to wear silver heels or flats, perhaps ones you already own, to give a little shine to your look.

Keep an eye out for seasonal shoe sales, especially at department stores, and visit discount shoe outlets to find an array of shoes for more than half off the price.

49. Find an Inexpensive Headpiece and Veil

Headpieces and veils bought at bridal salons are often quite costly, but you can ask to see their lower-priced designs, which may be simpler and without all of those pricey crystals and embroidery. Gown shops stock a variety of budget-priced headpieces and veils, but they may not have them on display in front-of-store display cases.

Simpler styles of veils and headpieces are usually lower-priced, and the benefit of a piece with no adornment—rather than thousands of crystals—is that you are the star of your look. Sometimes too much sparkle can look gaudy, and you don't need all that extra embellishment.

Remember that bridal salons need to unload last season's veils and headpieces, so they may have a sales rack, and their sample sales will often include these items for 50 to 70 percent off.

eBay and other auction sites are a great place to find these headpieces, including tiaras, both from bridal salons and from entrepreneurs who make them at home and then sell them online for less than retail prices.

Consignment shops are great places to find veils and head-pieces from brides who chose not to preserve them, or whose weddings were canceled. You may find $20 veils there.

Borrowing veils and headpieces is a great way to beat your budget, since a friend or relative will be honored to know she has such great taste that you would want to wear her choice on your own wedding day. That means your veil and headpiece would be free.

Or, you can make your own veil using an inexpensive kit from a crafts store. These $20 kits provide the materials you'll need—often already hemmed—with a headband and appliqués or other embellishments that you or a crafty friend could easily put together.

BRIDAL BONUS If you've been given a necklace by your fiancé or parents, you already have special jewelry to wear for the wedding. If you don't have something that seems ideal, a simple strand of pearls or a chain with a drop pearl is an elegant and risk-free option. You'll find items like these for any budget in the costume jewelry sections of department stores and other shops. If you usually prefer jewelry in a different style, don't spend the money for genuine pearls you may not wear very often.

Look at the style of your gown, as well. Your halter dress might mean you couldn't wear a necklace. Your embellished bodice might have enough sparkle in it so that you don't need drop earrings. A simpler jewelry look, again, makes you the star of your ensemble. You're not dripping in diamonds in what can be an overdone look.

CHAPTER 10

Set Your Beauty Budget

*E*very bride wants to beautiful on her big day—but if you're not careful, the bride's beauty budget can get out of hand very quickly. From finding knockoffs to learning DIY makeup tricks, you can follow these tips to save some room in your budget to share with everyone else at the wedding!

50. Arrange a Trial Run

Everyone has seen the bride who decides to use her wedding to try out a new look that just isn't her—whether it's a new hairstyle or just too much makeup. Ask your stylist to arrange a good time to get your haircut, body perm, or hair color so that it looks its best for your wedding. You don't want any unpleasant surprises on your wedding day! If your hair wilts or turns frizzy on a damp day, discuss a backup plan for a different style.

Do a test run with your stylist before the wedding, taking your veil, flowers, or whatever headpiece you're using with you. It's also a good idea to bring a photo of your wedding dress so you can both agree on a look that suits you best.

These test runs are often priced low, and sometimes they are free as part of the package you've booked to have your hair done on your wedding day. A freebie is always a great budget-saver.

51. Do Your Own Makeup

Think about consulting with a makeup expert at a counter in an upscale department store for advice on what colors and type of makeup to wear for different times of the day or season. You'll get some free advice on what looks good. Just be careful not to go overboard and buy expensive makeup you won't use again.

Plenty of brides practice before the wedding and then do their own makeup on the morning of the wedding. They don't need the professional makeup styling or the spray-on foundation, and they definitely don't need the special spray that sets makeup in what can look like a waxy coating of the face. Even better, you can use your own eyeliner, mascara, and lip gloss to avoid the problem of eye infections that can be caught through applicators that have been used on other people. Some brides say it was relaxing to do their own makeup on the wedding morning. It felt like getting ready for a big night out, and their own routine was grounding.

Another option is to ask a friend who is better at makeup application than you are to come to your place before the wedding to do your makeup for you. Your friend might be a cosmetologist whose makeup application is her wedding gift to you. You get a gorgeous look, always going for "natural, but a little bit better" for free.

CHAPTER 11

Money-Savers for the Groom and His Men

While the guys may not be paying the high amount of a wedding gown for their tux rentals, their expenses do add up! So here are some ways to help your groom and his men save a few bucks to get a special, attractive look for the wedding day.

52. Research Tuxedos

Who's looked at as much as the bride on the wedding day? Why, the groom, of course! And while he may be the handsomest man on the planet, some of the styles in the men's formalwear shop just don't cut it, do they? Some men look great in casual wear but look uncomfortable in a cutaway, and other men love a chance to look dashing in formalwear.

Glance through bridal magazines to get a sense of what type of men's formalwear is appropriate for the type of wedding you're having, and then consult with your local tuxedo-rental store. The biggest designers for men are Ralph Lauren, Tommy Hilfiger, Perry Ellis, and FUBU. Tuxes made by these designers are also available for sale.

The rules dictating what type of tux should be worn at which time of day are no longer operative. Just like women, men are refusing to be ruled by fashion tyrants. Wearing a tux is not even necessary. A simple, good-quality suit in black or dark gray (even brown for summer) is appropriate for many weddings. If you're having a Western wedding, for example, then you might want to go with a Texas formal style: tuxedo jackets with new jeans and a Stetson hat.

A visit to eBay might encourage your fiancé to buy a tux rather than rent one. Men's sizes tend to be more consistent than women's, so sizing shouldn't be much of a problem. If attending more formal events is in your future together, it makes more financial sense to buy a tux rather than rent one.

Sit down with your fiancé and take a look at some of the websites that feature tuxedo-rental stores. Good ones to check out are *www.afterhours.com* and *www.marryingman.com*. The latter flashes you a reminder of how many days left until "the Big Day" and encourages grooms to "Do It Now"—order the tux, that is!). You can look through the sites together and see what styles and colors would be appropriate for your wedding.

Ask if solid-colored vests and ties cost less than patterned ones, since some designers charge more for extra flair. And you might wish to skip the cummerbunds, since that's often too prom-like a look. The guys often look better in vests and ties.

Dress the Groomsmen for Less

In general, the tuxes for the groomsmen should be similar in style to the groom's tux. If the groom is going very formal, then it follows that the groomsmen need to be styled similarly. Likewise, if the wedding is more informal, the attire worn should be informal like the groom's.

Following the style set by the groom, the groomsmen need shirts and cummerbunds or vests that match those of the groom. Bow ties or regular ties should also match. Tuxedo-rental shops can take care of the whole package for the groomsmen: tuxedo, cummerbunds or vests, and shoes.

Groomsmen have more leeway when it comes to timing. They don't absolutely need to place their orders until two or three months before the wedding, but it helps to place the order early. No one wants to find himself competing for a tux with the local high school prom-goers.

Generally, all men in the wedding party order their formalwear from the same store to make certain that their look is consistent. Some stores also offer a discount package, granting a percentage off for large groups of men, usually six or more.

53. Find Groom's Discounts

Look out for discounts for the groom. The groom's tuxedo may come free if the groomsmen rent their tuxes from the same rental place. The groom might also be given free shoe rental, as the MVP of the wedding party.

> **WATCH OUT** Be aware that there could be surcharges if the groom or his groomsmen order their tuxes less than four weeks before the wedding, so keep timing in mind.

54. Save with Suits

Again, tuxes aren't strictly necessary. If you are having an informal wedding, opt for blazers instead of tuxes. You can rent suits or ask each groomsman to wear one he already owns. The groomsmen will also appreciate wearing their own season-appropriate suits to a less formal wedding, saving on the cost of the tuxedo rental.

Tie the look together with matching ties or pocket squares.

55. Decide on Informal Outfits

For extremely informal weddings, groomsmen can even forget the blazer. Ask them to wear khakis, and buy matching button-front shirts to distinguish them as groomsmen. Look at discount men's clothing shops, outlets, and department store sales and encourage the men to shop at these lower-priced sources to save themselves some extra money.

The groom can help his groomsmen save by not requiring that they rent their dress shoes from the tuxedo rental store, something the store personnel will try to emphasize they must do for a good look. Of course, you want a uniform look, so ask men to wear shined black shoes and black socks if they will wear a dark suit, or specify "no flip-flops" at an informal wedding. Guys can also find well-priced footwear at discount shoe stores and department stores so that they look well put-together for the wedding.

CHAPTER 12

Buy Budget Bridesmaid Dresses

*B*efore you ask those attendants to be part of your day, it's important to take a look at your budget. While the bride and groom are not responsible for paying for the attire of their wedding party, you still have to consider your finances. At the very least, each attendant means a bouquet or boutonniere, a meal at the rehearsal dinner and at the reception, transportation expenses to the reception, and a gift for participating.

Then, too, it's important for the bride and groom to think about how expenses may add up for their attendants. Each attendant must pay for the dress or the rental tux, special shoes, and accessories. There may be transportation costs and possibly even hotel stays. Attendants may have to miss work to attend the events or at the very least, time to attend rehearsals and so on. Therefore, it's important for the bride and groom to carefully look at budgets—both theirs and those of their prospective attendants.

New brides are the best source of advice for planning your wedding. If you know anyone who's recently gotten married or is a few months ahead of you in planning a wedding, ask her where she bought her bridesmaid dresses. You'll get recommendations and possibilities you might not have thought of.

56. Research Styles

Bridesmaids are the bride's attendants, the prelude to her walk down the aisle, a part of her inner circle on her special day. They deserve to look and feel their best. So this requires time spent researching the current dress trends, both online and at bridal shops, to see what's out there and how much these dresses cost.

Even if every bridesmaid wears the same dress size, they will each have different physical shapes and skin tones. So choosing the right dresses for the bridesmaids can be a daunting task. Finding identical dresses that look right on different persons takes attention on top of everything else you have to decide. Often the bride chooses a color scheme for her wedding that becomes the color range for the bridesmaid gowns.

First, Pick the Color

Seasons dictate certain colors. For spring, colors like pastel pinks, blues, greens, and yellows are popular, while summer colors are stronger and more vibrant. Fall colors deepen into more earthy tones like golds, russets, and browns. Winter colors include reds and greens, silver and gold, purple, and darker blues. And black? Black is a year-round favorite. It can be used even in summer for a dramatic, sophisticated bridal-attendant dress. White is another possibility, but many brides shun it for their attendants since they will wear it as the traditional center of attention. No matter what the season, using your favorite color is always a rewarding choice.

Look at the Style

One of the reasons bridesmaid gowns have been so hated is that they look like bridesmaid gowns. The idea these days is to make the dress something that can be worn again. Try not to choose something that's fussy, with big puffy sleeves or skirt or something that obviously labels it as a dress that was worn for a wedding.

The style of the bride's gown often determines that of her attendants. If you're wearing a sleek, floor-length sheath, try to pick bridesmaid gowns that mirror your look. Wearing an A-line gown? That can be the gown style you seek for your maid of honor and bridesmaids.

Consider your bridesmaids' body types, and choose a style that suits all of them. Remember, you aren't shopping for yourself. If you're small-chested and can pull off a strapless dress with minimal bra support, keep in mind that your future sister-in-law and her 36Ds may not thank you for picking that style.

A-line gowns basically look like the letter A: fitted bodice, natural waist, and flared skirt. They are flattering for almost every body type. Empire waists begin directly under a fitted bodice. Be aware that they can make heavier women look pregnant, although the style works for most bridesmaids.

Go bridesmaid-dress shopping with no more than one or two of your attendants at a time. The fewer people accompanying you, the easier it will be to reach a decision. Try to go with the bridesmaids most representative of your attendant group to get a sense of how different dresses will look on different people.

Or, let your bridesmaids know what color and/or style you have decided on and let each woman choose her own dress. You'll spend less time agonizing over finding a dress to suit everyone, and you won't have to deal with bridesmaids whining to you about how alarmingly fat they'll look in the dress you chose. Each bridesmaid will be able to pick the dress that suits her best, at her budget, and everyone will be happy.

Share the cost-cutting secrets you used for your own dress, and your bridesmaids will thank you.

57. Take Advantage of Seasonal Sales

You can find some great deals at the bridal salon where you bought your wedding gown. Sometimes, bridesmaid dress prices will be adjusted if your wedding gown is pricey or if you order a certain number of bridesmaid gowns. Ask about this when you go to buy your gown. Remember that if you're planning your wedding far in advance, your attendants can take advantage of end-of-season sales. Stick with a classic style and it won't be outdated when your wedding takes place.

For best selection, ask when the store gets its seasonal shipments. Many retail stores offer a discount when you open a store credit card, and this purchase is a good chance to take advantage of that opportunity.

58. Shop Prom Dresses and Formals

A bridesmaid dress doesn't have to have "bridesmaid" written on the tag or be located in the bridesmaid section of your wedding salon. Try looking in the prom section of department stores. Prom dresses haven't looked sweet and innocent in many years. Today's prom dresses are smart and stylish and are well suited to women over high school age. Start looking in March to find the best, new bridesmaid dresses, and look again in May when most prom-shopping is finished, and remaining dresses are on sale for up to 40 percent off, if not more.

Evening wear can double as bridesmaid wear. You'll find dresses of every description that can be wonderful for a wedding. Look for simple, classic designs, and let the saleswoman know you want the dresses for your bridesmaids. She'll be able to guide you to appropriate styles—nothing too revealing or too sexy. Some evening gowns come with matching jackets or wraps, which is a nice bonus, especially if the outfit is to be worn in the cooler months.

If you have fewer bridesmaids, you may find the perfect dresses on sale at regular department store formals sections. With just one or two bridesmaids to outfit, their sizes may be available right there on the rack, and you won't have to order from a pricey salon.

Check *www.outletbound.com* to find nearby outlet stores, including those from formalwear designers and share this information with your bridesmaids.

Some bridesmaids who live in regions of the country where clothing is priced lower will take on the task of getting bridesmaids' sizes and buying the dresses near their home, for a savings of 20 percent or more.

59. Save Them Money on Shoes

Shoes are a challenge. For a uniform look, you can pick out one pair of shoes and ask each bridesmaid to buy a pair in her size. This means more work for you, unfortunately, and some bridesmaids might grumble about style, comfort, and price.

For a semi-uniform look, you can ask your bridesmaids to wear a certain color and allow them to pick their own shoes. Try to pick a color your bridesmaids will wear again. Metallic shades such as silver and gold are popular, and they are appropriate for many bridesmaid dresses. Let bridesmaids know about the discount shoe stores or shoe outlets you found for your own wedding day shoes, and they too can enjoy lower prices.

You can also help keep costs down by letting your attendants wear their own dress-appropriate shoes. Some brides want their attendants to wear dyed-to-match shoes, which can be expensive as well as not always a color they will wear again. How often will you wear a pair of peach-toned satin shoes or a pair of strappy silver sandals with three-inch heels if you're a casual kind of girl?

60. Find Budget-Friendly Accessories

Shawls, stoles, and wraps can be a lovely accessory for a wedding—and a necessity if you get married on a chilly day. If you're having the attendants' gowns made, buy extra fabric and have matching wraps sewn. The cost will be low, but the look will be rich. Retail stores tend to place wraps on sale after holidays and proms. Your attendants will thank you, especially if their gowns are strapless or have spaghetti straps. Even the young and toned don't always like their shoulders and arms.

BRIDAL BONUS Add gorgeous satin sashes—maybe even tie one on your wedding gown—or try some metallic belts. Jeweled appliqués are simple to sew on for drama and are budget friendly, too. Add brooches or pins for just a touch of sparkle to punch up a dull dress.

Sample sales can outfit your bridesmaids as well as you, so you might want to bring your maid of honor along to check out the accessories your maids might be willing to wear for half-price.

Check out the jewelry in teen accessory stores at the mall, and at Target, WalMart, or other discount stores for pretty, simple silver or colored jewelry that can be yours for under $10 apiece. Some stores offer two-for-one sales that will cut the jewelry prices by 50 percent.

CHAPTER 13

Find Budget Deals for Child Attendants

*I*s there anything more adorable than the smallest members of the wedding party? We're talking precious little girls all dressed up, their hair styled in "princess" hairdos, walking down the aisle scattering rose petals. Then there are those handsome little boys in miniature tuxes carrying the wedding rings tied to a ring pillow.

While you can never be quite sure about how they'll behave that day—they are, after all, children—you can depend on having them be a very special part of your day. Since parents have enough expenses, they'll appreciate your help in keeping down the costs of the clothing.

61. Shop Smart

You can find flower-girl and junior-bridesmaid dresses in a bridal store, of course, but also in the regular children's section of a department store, especially at holiday time. A dress that's displayed for a Christmas party can be wonderful for a wedding, too. Ask the parent to buy the dress in the size she anticipates the child will be when the wedding takes place. Prices for holiday dresses, especially through after-holiday sales, can reflect a significant savings of up to 70 percent off. You'll also find a great array of kids' party dresses and suits around the time of first Communions and during the Easter holidays. Again, post-holiday sales can net you big savings. Pageant stores can also be a source of dresses for a flower girl. Let parents know about outlet stores, so that they can cash in on big savings.

Or go online for auctions. eBay and other online auctions are an invaluable source of formalwear for little girls and boys. The clothing has usually been worn just one time. Some bridal-wear and formalwear stores also sell new items online. Either way, the seller must state whether the clothing is new or used. Remember that you can always have clothing professionally dry-cleaned if you buy it used.

62. Add Twists to Their Party Clothes

Looks for children tend to stay in style for a long time. You would be safe, for instance, in using a dress worn in a wedding a few years earlier, perhaps by a sibling or a cousin. Some dresses can even be dyed a different color for a fresh look. Try adding a new sash in a color to match the bridal attendants or sew some silk flowers or sparkly trim on an old dress to add charm. Sash material and embellishments are super-cheap at craft stores.

Ring-bearer tuxedo rentals are often very low-priced, such as $20 to $30 for the little guys. Some parents like to dress their boys in their own black pants, and just buy a white shirt that matches the groomsmen. For a more casual look, you can buy a regular suit at a department store or let the ring bearer wear a suit he already owns. Buy him a tie to match the groomsmen so that he'll fit right in.

63. Find Bargains on Baskets and Pillows

Bridal salons strategically lay out flower-girl baskets and ring-bearer pillows for brides to notice when they shop for themselves. However, you can easily save money by buying or making these items yourself.

You'll find baskets in all sizes at any craft store, which you can spray-paint whatever color you like and then attach ribbons to the handles to make them fancier. For a variation of the traditional flower-girl image, you can forgo the basket and let your flower girl carry a mini-bouquet or pomander.

Making your own pillow for your ring bearer ensures that you save money and get the design you like the best. You can pick the fabric and color you prefer and accent it with ribbons or appliqués. A homemade ring pillow might cost $5, while a store-bought one might cost $30. There's no rule that says the ring bearer needs a pillow, either. You can have him carry the rings in a jewelry box you inherited from your great-grandmother or another piece that has a special significance for you or your fiancé.

PART V

Find Savings on

Wedding Essentials

CHAPTER 14

Save on Invitations and Print Items

Choosing and ordering invitations is one of the most exciting parts of wedding planning. Now that you've decided on a time, date, and location for your wedding, finally seeing the details in print can give you an exciting feeling that it's really going to happen. But the prices! It can be hard to believe that paper and ink can add up to hundreds of dollars, but there's a lot that goes into invitation design that affects the prices. Here, you'll find out how to get the perfect print look for less.

64. Select Inexpensive Save-the-Dates

Formerly reserved exclusively for guests who needed to travel long distances or for weddings scheduled on holiday weekends, save-the-dates are an increasingly popular way of getting the word out about your wedding, no matter when it is or who is invited. Some stationery retailers offer discounts for couples who buy both their save-the-dates and invitations at the same place.

Save-the-date cards don't necessarily have to be actual cards. Creative couples order save-the-date magnets so their guests can remember the upcoming event every time they get milk out of the refrigerator. They can cost as little as fifty cents per magnet.

Save-the-dates are usually sent six months before the wedding. A piece of paper mailed with your names, your wedding date, and your wedding location might seem like a frivolous waste of money, but it can help your guests start planning all of their travel arrangements. You can also use this as an opportunity to pass along information about local hotels, discount rates, and wedding attire either on the notice or by mentioning the URL of your personal wedding website.

> **WATCH OUT** When you add up save-the-date notices, invitations, and response cards, postage will be a significant expense. Be sure it's included in your budget. If you don't figure it in, you will think you're on target with your budget, but when you sit down to add everything up—ouch!

One inexpensive option is to send digital save-the-dates to your guests' e-mail addresses. Wedding websites such as The Knot (*www.theknot.com*) offer free electronic save-the-dates.

If you prefer physical save-the-date cards, consider designing them yourself and printing them on your home computer. The only expenses will be paper, ink, and postage.

65. Choose Less Expensive Invitations

Let your wedding style and budget guide you as you pick out your wedding invitations. Your invitations let your guests catch a glimpse of your wedding's style and degree of formality.

You want your invitation to be different from everyone else's, but you also don't want to spend a lot of money. Stay with the least expensive cardstock and printing options, and then add your own unique features with a special or customized sealing stamp or ribbon that you can attach yourself.

Single-panel invitations often cost less than fancy tri-page invitation booklets or tri-fold papers.

A classic style with just black lettering will usually cost less than invitations with pearlized borders or raised graphics. Also, the designer you choose might translate into higher prices.

Be mindful of your budget when ordering the number of invitations, too. It's best to order an additional two-dozen invitations in case you suddenly remember guests you should have invited or if you make a mistake filling out envelopes. Get your count right. No one wants to have to go back to the printer with a small order and pay for express service or express mail.

66. Order at Discount Sources

Start by finding stationery suppliers. You can visit local stationery suppliers or opt for virtual shopping. Websites offer a multiplicity of invitation styles, prices, and creative touches to suit any budget. Just type "wedding invitations" into your favorite search engine and links to hundreds of sites will appear, many of which offer the same name brands carried by the best stationery stores. Prices can be anywhere from 15 to 30 percent lower than those from a local store, though be sure to consider shipping costs in dealing with an online stationery service. Visit *www.invitations4sale.com* for a range of top-name invitations at 40 percent off.

If you're unsure of what you want, certain wedding websites and bridal-magazine sites show galleries of wedding invitations. Free catalogs and samples are available, and many companies offer to send you a proof of your invitation to make sure you're totally happy before you complete your order.

67. Make Your Own Invitations

You can make your own wedding invitations. Buy kits at office-supply or stationery stores and design them at home. All you need is a little time and a good printer—no artistic ability required. You can design your own invitations using a word processing program, then print them out and assemble them. Invitation kits come with everything you need, including response cards and envelopes. Paper Source (*www.papersource .com*) has unique kits and ideas for do-it-yourself invitations.

Check your craft store for DIY invitation kits, and comparison-shop. Some brand-name kits are far more expensive than others. Office supply stores also offer invitation-making software and kits, which can add up to big savings when you use them to create all of the print items you need, such as menu cards and place cards.

> **BRIDAL BONUS** Some couples include their e-mail addresses on their invitations, allowing guests to R.S.V.P. electronically. People are so busy these days, it's often easier for them to respond by e-mail. Personalized wedding websites give you the option to let guests respond online, too, so you might choose not to order or make response cards or need extra postage for them.

68. Avoid Embellishments

Remember that options that make your invitations fancier, such as special trims like lace or appliqués or specialty papers, add to the expense and may require additional postage.

CHAPTER 15

Save on Flowers

*W*eddings and flowers—they just go together. Many of us remember the flowers from weddings we've attended: the fragrant white roses of the bride's bouquet, the garden wedding site that's a symphony of color and scent, the little baskets of lily of the valley at the reception tables.

Flowers can make a wedding. They can also break your budget if you're not careful. How much you choose to spend and what portion of the budget you allot is totally up to you. Some sources suggest that flowers are the second-biggest expense after reception food and drink, but they don't have to be. If flowers aren't a high priority for you, set a smaller budget for them and spend your money where you want to.

69. Trim Expenses with Your Floral Order

Map out exactly where you want flowers. If the site of either the ceremony or reception is in an already lavishly decorated space, you may need few if any floral arrangements. If you do need them for both locales, figure out whether the flowers from the ceremony can be taken to the reception site as well. You also need to decide what to do about bouquets, boutonnieres, and corsages. If you decide to forgo the bouquets, you and your bridesmaids can walk down the aisle with fans or parasols. Consider making the boutonnieres for the groom, groomsmen, and fathers yourself.

You need flowers for the setting of your wedding ceremony. If you're using a large church or synagogue, flower and ribbon decorations on the pews can really add up in cost. Decide whether you want to have a decoration on each pew, every other pew, or none at all. Figure out the cost differences between simple and elaborate choices, and then you'll know which you want.

70. Research Flowers

Many people are all thumbs with flowers and barely know the names of different plants. Such people are happy to leave flower designing and arranging to the florist, but even florists need direction to ensure you're happy with the final product. Here are some ideas you might like to consider.

- Look up shapes. One bride looked through several issues of bridal magazines to get an idea of the kinds of flowers and bouquet shapes available during her wedding season. She learned the difference between a cascade bouquet, an arm bouquet, a nosegay, and a pomander. Her familiarity with the terminology saved time when she went to the florist and kept her from having unrealistic expectations.
- Add seasonal elements to your centerpieces. In addition to using seasonal flowers to keep prices down, pay tribute to the time of year by incorporating small buds in the spring or colorful leaves in the autumn.Seasonal weddings give you lots of ideas for inexpensive decorating. An added bonus is that many of the places you'll use for a ceremony or reception site will be decorated for the season, which translates into less decorating and less money on your end!
- Investigate *www.blissezine.com*, a website with a floral guide that tells you types of flowers, their colors, and available seasons. It also helps to know the names of particular flowers and good substitutes for more expensive flowers than your budget will allow.

71. Find Florist Savings

To find a florist you will be pleased with, get referrals from others. Ask past customers whether the flowers they ended up with were the ones they had ordered. Make sure there were no unexpected, expensive add-ons.

When you have your preliminary list, try to visit two or three florists before making a choice. Ask lots of questions about what you want, and pay attention to how you're treated. If the florist is not willing to spend a few minutes discussing what you want, you have not found the vendor for you.

Come prepared with pictures of bouquets and arrangements you like that you've clipped from magazines, and ask whether the florist can duplicate the look. If you feel patted on the head and gently encouraged to choose from a few photos of standard bouquets or a prepackaged floral-arrangement album, you're in the wrong place.

Ask to see pictures of the flowers the florist has done for past weddings, which will give you an idea of the florist's style. Even if this doesn't match your own, a good florist is still able to make your vision a reality. Tell him what you have in mind for your wedding and ask whether he has any suggestions. Ask him how he will approach your wedding and whether you will be able to see advance samples of your bouquets and arrangements.

The final step is to make certain you get the transaction details in writing. You should have a written agreement spelling out the price of the flowers and the style of the arrangements. Also put in writing when the florist will deliver the flowers for your ceremony and reception so there is no misunderstanding or excuse for undelivered flowers. Ask whether the florist will set the arrangements in place and stay to pin on boutonnieres and corsages.

72. Think Smaller

Carry a smaller bouquet both for a savings in the number of flowers needed to fill a big bouquet, and also to flatter your body size. A petite bride will look better carrying a smaller bouquet, rather than a larger one. Also, create smaller centerpieces, such as a half dozen peonies or roses low-set in a vase, instead of a big, dramatic centerpiece containing dozens of flowers. Big flowers can also save you money, since a centerpiece containing six big Gerber daisies will make a visual impact and cost less than a centerpiece containing two dozen roses. The fewer flowers you need, the lower the cost.

73. Use Alternative Flowers

Look outside of traditional bridal flowers, such as roses, gardenias, and stephanotis. Ask your floral designer to suggest non-wedding flowers such as peonies and tulips that are priced well, and not elevated in demand or expense if this is wedding season.

Weddings that have a medieval, Victorian, or Western flavor dictate their own color schemes and flowers. Ivy and wildflowers are evocative of medieval times, while rose and lace nosegays are suitable for a Victorian theme. Western brides take their inspiration from regional flowers and casual bouquet shapes.

Another alternative to save money is arranging small single decorations such as votive candles in glass holders or tiny flowerpots filled with blooms are inexpensive touches that add gaiety to any wedding. They can also serve double duty as party favors. For modest budgets, look in dollar stores for cute little flowerpots and votives in bundles of one hundred. These items are also on sale at craft stores and discount superstores. For moderate-budget weddings, look in department stores for fancier glass votive holders and candles. For truly lavish weddings, think about bowls with floating candles every few place settings on the tables.

74. Give Flowers Double-Duty

"We also saved having the flowers taken from the church and sent on to the reception site," says one bride. "That was a service that the florist suggested, something I hadn't thought of, and it helped us save the expense of ordering additional flowers for the reception site."

If you like the look of flower petals for your aisle runner or as table décor, ask your florist if he or she would be willing to use petals from any extra roses in your existing order, or the petals from extra stock in the florist shop. You may be able to get these petals for free.

75. Design Single-Flower Bouquets and Centerpieces

Rather than a full bouquet, carry a single white rose tied at the stem with a ribbon for a pretty, elegant look. Other flowers to consider for single-stem bouquets and centerpieces include red roses, calla lilies, Gerber daisies, bird of paradise for an island wedding, and other big dramatic flowers.

Find tall glass vases at the craft store or dollar store and create your own centerpieces by placing one, pretty flower in each, sprinkling those free rose petals on the table around that centerpiece.

76. Design Boutonnieres and Corsages for Less

Don't forget to budget for corsages for the mothers and grand-mothers. Many brides order corsages with flowers similar to those in their bridal bouquets, but if you know your mother or your fiancé's mother loves a particular flower, you might want to incorporate it if it's not too expensive or out of season. While some florists will show you dramatic corsages or wrist-lets made with three or four flowers, or expensive orchids, keep it simple with a smaller arrangement that doesn't overpower the mom's style.

Boutonnieres can be expensive if you get too fancy with the variety of flowers or with the arrangement. Most men gener-ally prefer just a small, simple flower—one like those from the bride's bouquet—pinned to their lapel, anyway. Again, stick with in-season flowers, avoid imported flowers, and skip the addition of multiple filler flowers. All the guys need is just one rose or sprig of stephanotis.

77. Plan for Kids' Flowers

Kids may carry baskets filled with rose petals to scatter, so again ask if you can get those petals for free as part of your floral package.

If kids will be wearing flowers as a wreath, keep the design simple with just three or four roses at the crown and filler flowers or greenery on the rest of the circle to cut the cost by over 50 percent. The little ones are so adorable on their own; they really don't need added floral touches. But you can order small nosegay bouquets for the flowergirls to carry, which due to their tiny size may cost a third of the cost of the bridesmaids' flowers.

78. Find Alternative Flower Sources

Wholesale outlets like Costco sell flowers in bulk at a discount. You can order live flowers ahead of time and pick them up before your wedding. You can rent or buy inexpensive vases or bowls and assemble your centerpieces yourself. Other sources of inexpensive flowers include:

- Supermarket garden departments, with potted mini roses for just $3.

- A floral wholesaler, which you can find online. Check out *www.fiftyflowers.com* as an example.
- Garden centers and nurseries during their seasonal sales.
- Family farms, which may offer organic flowers at half the price.
- If you need only a few flowers for a bouquet and décor for a small wedding, why not grow your own? In advance of your wedding date, plant the types of flower bushes you'll need and snip the blooms you wish to use for the wedding. Parents and friends may be willing to let you cut flowers and greenery from their property as well.

79. Dream Up DIY Savings

If you'd like to do any part of the flower arrangements yourself, find a wholesaler like Costco or visit a flower market or flea market for bargains. Look for locally grown varieties for the best savings. Rent vases from local florists or buy inexpensive ones from the dollar store. Do a test run before the wedding to make sure you feel comfortable assembling a flower arrangement.

If you want to save money on flowers but feel clueless when it comes to working with real or silk flowers, don't despair. Ready-made arrangements are available at many decorating stores; some even have designers who can make what you want from silk flowers and greenery you purchase at the store.

The charge, is usually reasonable compared to ordering from a florist.

Martha Stewart Weddings magazine demystifies the process of making your own simple bouquets. Check out *www .marthastewart.com/weddings* for more information on wedding flowers and other features designed to help you have a stylish and affordable wedding.

A flower-arranging class could come in useful for making your bouquets and centerpieces.

Look online for helpful articles on making floral pieces for weddings, and see if your local library has instructional videos. You can also sign up for flower-arranging courses at local craft stores or through college campuses at a low price, usually including materials you'll need. A new trend is to fill a vase or glass container with fruit such as lemons or limes before inserting flowers. The use of ornamental branches or grasses can be striking. Grouping fall fruits and vegetables makes an appealing seasonal theme. If you're getting married near Christmas, go with stylish little trees on your table or figurines that spotlight the season.

Edible centerpieces are wonderfully tempting for guests. Apples in the fall and oranges in the summer are beautiful and tasty—just let your guests know they can eat the centerpieces if the urge strikes them.

Whatever the season, have lots of candles, little votives, or tea lights. Candlelight is wonderfully flattering and an inexpensive way of creating a luxe look. Check with your reception site to see whether there are any restrictions on candlelight before proceeding with your plans, and find candles and holders on the cheap at dollar and craft stores.

You can also group your favors as a centerpiece. Candy favors, even candy bars, are a popular feature at weddings today. Fill inexpensive glass-lidded jars with a variety of colorful candies, provide ladles and containers, and let guests scoop out their own candy. They can consume the candy right at the reception.

CHAPTER 16

Make Memorable Music

You'll want to arrange for fantastic music at your wedding, to set a tone, entertain your guests, and keep your dance floor filled. If you've already started researching the topic, you know that entertainment packages are very expensive. That's because the music can make or break the reception. Couples who booked the least expensive entertainers wound up with less-than-pleasing music. The key is to research well, find the right entertainers for your budget, and make the best plans possible for a budget that's music to your ears.

80. Find Great Musicians

The same rules apply for finding both ceremony and reception musicians. Make sure you check with your ceremony venue to find out what type of music they allow. In some locations, only taped music will be available or appropriate, but other places may require you to hire a live musician. If you are getting married in a religious setting, ask whether it's acceptable to stray from traditional pieces.

If you have a college or university in your area, even a small music school, you might be able to find musicians available there for your wedding and reception. Students are always in need of money for tuition and living expenses, and playing at a wedding gives them a chance to gain experience for their future careers.

Be sure to check the musicians' references and make certain that there is a backup plan in place if they are ill or can't make your event. Also offer to provide a reference for them if you're happy with their work.

While at church, ask if the organist would be available to play at your wedding, and at what price. The same goes for choirs and soloists who perform at the church.

Ask friends and family for recommendations. Who did they hire to play at their ceremony and reception. Your ceremony venue is also a good source of information, as are your additional wedding vendors who have worked with everyone in town. They will be able to suggest a well-priced, talented musician for your day.

Other brides and grooms have found talented performers at their local coffee shop, and they hired them to play the wedding for well under the price of professional groups.

81. Decide on a Deejay vs. a Band

An important consideration is whether you want the style of a deejay or a band. They both offer different tones with their music, and you may prefer one over the other as a rule. Keep in mind that deejays are usually less expensive than bands, due to the fact that there's only one expert in attendance, rather than a band's five or six people.

Finding an Entertainer in Your Budget Range

The website *www.WeDJ.com* is a useful resource for finding a deejay for your wedding. Simply click on your state and county, and you'll find lists of deejays in your area. The site lets you easily contact deejays and set up arrangements.

Deejays are versatile and can accommodate a wide range of musical tastes and requests. Live bands tend to be less flexible, but they can specialize in everything from oldies covers to swing tunes.

Bands usually have repertoires that span all kinds of music, and you can see them perform for free at bridal showcases. Some may even invite you to poke your head into a ballroom at a live wedding they're playing so that you can see how well they work the crowd.

Making Your Plans to Suit Your Budget

Plan on making a number of calls and talking to several bands or deejays to find one that can meet your musical needs and fit your budget. At each interview, first make sure the band or deejay is available on your date, then ask how soon you need to commit. Ask whether you will be charged by the job or by the hour. If you are charged one flat fee, ask how many hours the band or deejay will be available for you. Find out whether the time frame you are quoted includes setup and cleanup. Finally, make sure the band or deejay's style fits your own. Request a musical collection list from them, and submit your own playlist.

82. Depend on Your iPod Playlist

You can provide your own entertainment for free by loading your choice of songs onto your iPod, and setting it on a dock to play the music at your ceremony and your reception. You'll just create separate playlists for both, and you can further customize your songs by choosing music for the dinner hour and the dancing hour.

Make sure your iPod battery is fully charged before you get to the reception, and plug it in once you get there. Have a Plan B readily available in case your iPod fails you for any reason.

Hooking the iPod up to speakers at the reception is easy even for people not technically inclined, although there are a few caveats. Make sure your reception venue is set up to handle an iPod wedding. You may have to rent speakers that will work in the size of your venue. You can program your iPod ahead of time, but put a trusted friend or relative in charge of it. He can switch the music if the dance floor is too empty and prevent overenthusiastic guests from making unauthorized musical changes.

83. Plan Personal Performances

For an unforgettable personal touch at the ceremony and the reception, ask a talented friend or relative to perform a song for you. Perhaps you have a cousin who plays the piano. He can perform the music for your ceremony. If a friend is a singer, he or she can take the microphone from the deejay and sing a few songs to delight the crowd.

Some brides and grooms will even sing or perform songs themselves, as a gift or surprise for their new spouse.

These personal performances don't cost a thing, and even if they are just a snippet of your reception, it still saves you the high cost of booking a band for a live performance.

CHAPTER 17

Choose Transportation for Less

*T*ransportation to the church and reception contributes to the atmosphere of your day, whether you arrive in a limo or on a motorcycle. As soon as you booked your ceremony and reception sites, you probably determined what kind of wedding-day locomotion you need. If you require any special transportation other than your own two feet, arranging it can be enjoyable if you remember to use the same planning and budgetary concern you've applied to other elements of your wedding.

84. Practice Limousine Smarts

Many couples opt to rent a limousine to shuttle themselves and the wedding party around town.

Always get recommendations from friends, family, business associates, and your wedding vendors. Visit the company and talk to a representative about your needs and her prices, and ask to see her vehicles and a contract. Be sure to ask if any wedding packages are available and what they include.

Try to have most details worked out before you draw up a contract arranging transportation for the wedding and reception. The more specific you can be about matters up-front, such as times, tolls, number of people, and mileage, the fewer surprises you'll have later. And you may be able to save thousands if you know you only need a limousine to take you from the ceremony to the reception.

Most limos are contracted at an hourly rate, which will quickly add up during the ceremony and reception. Find out exactly when the time clock begins; there can be a big difference between a company that charges as soon as its car leaves the garage and one that waits until it arrives at your house. Ask how many hours you will have the limousine and what happens if you go over your time. If you live in a large city, make sure you know who is responsible for paying tolls and parking charges. Make sure to budget for a gratuity, which can sometimes be as high as 20 percent. Be sure all these points are included in writing in your contract.

Another factor to keep in mind is that a regular limo will cost less than a stretch limo, and a black limo may cost less than a white limo. Ask the company representative to explain these differences in price, and you may find additional savings together.

85. Look into Alternative Transportation

Here are some alternative forms of transportation that can often be rented at low prices:

- Trolleys
- Horse-drawn carriage
- Taxicabs
- Yachts or boats (especially if a friend has one you can use for free!)
- Golf carts

86. Use Your Own Car

This one is free! Decorate your own car, or a friend's car, with soap-based paints and bridal-themed signs—which you can't do with a limousine—and take a personally chauffeured ride to and from your wedding. If a friend has a convertible or sporty car he or she wouldn't mind driving on your wedding day, perhaps this friend can provide your mode of transportation as a wedding gift to you.

Before the wedding, have the exterior and interior of the car cleaned to make for better photos and prevent your gown from getting stained or dirty. Some couples lay a clean sheet over the seats to protect the gown and tux further.

Family members can follow your lead, decorate their own cars, and enjoy a safe and comfortable ride to the wedding, rather than needing limousines or other cars rented for the day.

BRIDAL BONUS The hotel where guests are staying will probably have a free shuttle that will take them to and from the wedding, and even to and from the airport. Arrange with the hotel sales manager to provide this free ride for your guests, and you may be able to hop on the shuttle with your guests to get to your wedding night suite! This would prevent you from needing extra hours of limousine rental for the end of the evening, at a savings of hundreds of dollars. You would just need the limo to take you to the ceremony and to the reception site, which can cost you half the price of a full package.

CHAPTER 18

Arrange Photography and Videography for Less

The photos and video from your wedding are of the utmost importance, since they are the only tangible reminders of your big day. As such, photographers and videographers charge a lot of money for their services. You do have a lot of options when it comes to arranging for budget-friendly photos and videos, so read on to find out the best plans to make.

87. Get Referrals

Ask your friends and family members whether they mind telling you what prices they paid for their wedding photography and whether proofs were delivered when expected. Make sure the photographer did not tack on extra hidden fees or try to charge for services that weren't in the contract, such as touchups.

Gather recommendations from your wedding vendors and wedding coordinator to find the best-priced pros in the area, and then plan to visit with them, see their samples, and review their price packages. Most will provide a basic budget package, which you'll find will meet all of your needs. Higher-priced packages often contain more prints, albums, and special effects than you need.

Another alternative is to think locally. Many colleges and universities have photography departments or programs. You might be able to locate a skilled instructor or student who does weddings.

It's essential to determine that the person you interview is the one who will be your photographer later. Developing a rapport with a photographer who turns out not to be yours can lead to disappointment if the quality of the product is less than you expected.

88. Choose Smaller Packages

Don't feel obliged to give away lots of wedding pictures to your family and friends. Share your photos on your wedding website or attach them to e-mails. If these aren't options, let your family and friends know how they can order copies from your photographer.

If a grand album of wedding photographs isn't a high-priority item in your wedding budget, then scale down the photography package. Ask the photographer to take fewer shots and develop fewer pictures. See whether it's possible for him to cover fewer hours than he normally would.

For a modest budget, choose a less ornate album and fewer posed shots that take a lot of time to compose. Larger photography packages and complex shots increase the price. Photography packages differ in the number of hours covered, the number of shots taken, and the way your photos are delivered. You can order your photos à la carte, in an album, or in a coffee-table photo book.

With your videographer, you can arrange for only one camera to be used, rather than the option of two to three cameras giving you different angles for editing later. Often, just the one camera will capture all the action.

Limit the number of special effects you want, if any, so that you're not paying a fortune in the videographer's post-production work. Some couples just ask for the raw tape of the day's footage, and they plan to have it professionally edited later, either by a pro or using their own home computer.

And for both photographer and videographer who offer by-the-hour packages, you can save a fortune by cutting your cake earlier in the reception, which means you can release these pros an hour or two earlier, for fewer hours of service.

89. Skip Professional Albums

Don't choose a package that contains professionally created, leather-bound albums or edited scrapbook style albums that include hundreds of photos in a flipbook. You can take your free proofs, along with photos that other people take on your big day, and fill your own albums that you've found inexpensively at the craft store. This is a great option for parents' albums if you feel you do want a professional album for yourselves.

WATCH OUT Beware of well-intentioned but inexperienced family members who have just bought a new videotape recorder and can't wait to use it. Sure, they can bring it to the wedding and make a video for themselves, but do you really want to rely on Uncle Joe for your wedding video? Only you know the answer to that question.

90. Plan DIY Photos and Video

You need not restrict yourself to professional photographers. If someone in your family wants to take photos and you like her work, accept her offer, though only if you truly believe she will do a great job. This occasion is too important to risk getting amateur-quality work.

If you've released your professional photographer early, have guests take candids using one-time-use cameras that you've bought in bulk from the craft store or at a warehouse store. You'll save a lot of money by avoiding those on bridal websites.

CHAPTER 19

Finding Favors and Gifts on a Budget

edding favors add a warm touch to a wedding reception. Many couples like to give a small heartfelt gift for their guests to take home as a memento of the wedding. Sometimes the favors serve double duty as a decorative touch on a reception table, such as silver frames that double as place-card holders.

91. Find the Best Place to Shop

You know that craft stores are a great source of inexpensive party needs, and you'll find candleholders, frames, and other favors for less than $2 apiece.

Visit *www.kateaspen.com* to find seasonal and theme favors for less, and look at bridal websites' clearance pages for bulk buys at a steal.

If your budget is strained, it is acceptable to skip the favors altogether. Ultimately, your guests attend your wedding to share your joy, not to collect a matchbook with your name on it.

The selection of candy favors is endless, and you'll find great prices at bulk candy stores where you scoop your chosen candies into a bag and pay by the pound. Eco-weddings are becoming more popular, and couples can give tiny tree seedlings and know that something from their day will grow in the years to come. Flower seeds are also popular favors at low prices. Some companies print the names of the bride and groom and their wedding date on packets of seeds.

Wedding gifts for attendants fall into two categories: those they can use on the day of the wedding and those that are everyday useful items. Deciding on the category is as important as how much you spend.

Gifts your bridesmaids can use at the wedding include jewelry, handbags, dressy headbands, earring and necklace sets, or baskets filled with items for pampering, such as aromatherapy candles, foaming bath salts, fancy bath sponges, manicure sets, or a novel to read in the tub, and after-bath body lotion. You can buy ready-made packages or assemble them yourself by choosing items that fit your budget.

A vase is a practical gift that can be used to hold blossoms either at home or the office. Personalize it with a gold or silver craft pen or use a kit to do faux engraving on the glass. A little frame with a picture of your attendant and you is a nice present from one friend to another. Or you can give small memorable photo albums.

Groomsmen can get some use on the day of the wedding out of a set of cuff links. However, a new tie might be a better choice if you want the recipient to wear it more often. A men's manicure set or small travel bag is also a handy gift. Alcohol-themed gifts like beer-can holders, drinking glasses, pub signs, and flasks are other popular choices, often found for sale on bridal websites and at *www.thingsremembered.com*.

92. Make Your Own Gifts

Don't feel you have to outdo the last wedding you went to with your favors. If you're creative and have the time, make something that only you can do. No time or all thumbs at crafts? You'll find plenty of ideas for favors that come ready-made.

Making your own favors can save you money and add a special personalized touch to your wedding day. This task doesn't have to be a solitary endeavor. You can enlist your fiancé or a few friends and make a party out of assembling favors. Some ideas include potpourri, scented oils, decorative soaps, and personalized candles using kits found cheaply at the craft store.

The easiest wedding favor to make is a candy favor—and just to be clear, you're not making the candy yourself! Present your guests with a handful of colorful mints or foil-wrapped chocolates.

Jordan almonds are perennial wedding favorites. They come in white, pastels, black, and even silver and gold foil-wrapped white almonds. Almonds are a symbol of life, and the sugared coating a wish that bride and groom have more sweetness than bitterness in their lives together. A charming candy-favor idea is to wrap five almonds in a tulle circle, twist, and tie a ribbon around the bundle. The number is symbolic, representing health, wealth, happiness, fertility, and longevity.

Hershey's Kisses and Hugs are always popular. Simply wrap a few chocolates in tulle or place them in a little favor box. Favor boxes come in more shapes and sizes and prices than you can imagine, and adorable favor bags and boxes are quite inexpensive at the craft store. You can also make your own personalized labels on your home computer and printer.

PART VI

Handling Additional

Expenses

CHAPTER 20

Save Money on Extras

Those additional expenses add up! You already know to have a budget for unexpected bills, so keep the following categories in mind so that you don't have to dip into your personal savings to meet them.

93. Hand Out Tips

It's prudent to thank all of the people who worked hard and dedicated their time to making your wedding such a memorable experience with a monetary tip. Keep track of tips carefully! Some gratuities may be built into your contract, especially for duties such as catering, and tipping some vendors may not be necessary. Here are the going rates for tipping:

- Wedding Officiant. If the officiant of your wedding ceremony is a member of the clergy, find out the fee you're expected to pay. Don't assume that officiating at your wedding is part of her salary. Weddings are not considered part of regular duties, meaning the officiant should be compensated. If the officiant doesn't want to name a figure, ask some friends or family members who have been recently married what they paid. Think about what an important role this person is performing for you. If a fee is not accepted, then make an appropriate donation to the church or synagogue. Civil officials who perform a wedding might not be allowed to charge for their services. Check before the wedding to see whether there is a fee and how much it is.

- Caterers, wait staff, and bartenders. Check your contract. Gratuities may be included, but make sure they cover the entire staff. If they don't, decide on a flat dollar amount for each member of the wait staff.

- Delivery people. You do not need to tip the florist or the baker, but you should tip the people who deliver the finished products in one piece to the reception site.

- Photographer and videographer. Use your discretion. Photographers and videographers don't always expect a tip, but this is a nice way to thank the people who develop your priceless images.

- Deejays and band members. This is up to you. If the deejay has a partner or there are multiple band members, figure a flat rate per person and deliver the tip to the leader.

- Limousine driver. A gratuity may be built into your contract, so check before you hand out the cash.

- Parking and coatroom attendants. These helpers should receive $1 per car or coat.

- Makeup artists and hair stylists. You normally leave a tip when you get your hair cut, so a hairdo for your wedding requires an even greater tip.

- Wedding coordinator. Say thank you to the person who introduced you to all of the other vendors.

If you find that certain vendors for your wedding provide excellent service, consider writing them a note or offering a recommendation or reference. Some vendors also have a section for testimonials on their websites. It's nice for a professional to be appreciated, and it's doubly nice when hard work pays off in future business.

BRIDAL BONUS The general rule for tipping is 10 to 15 percent of the total charge and up to 20 percent if the service is exceptional.

94. Be Smart with Insurance

You don't want to think about it, but it has to be said. Things happen. That's why many couples consider wedding insurance. A wedding is actually one of the biggest investments you will ever make; many couples spend more on their wedding than they would for an automobile or a trip abroad. Logically, then, wedding insurance might be a good idea.

You've been charging everything on a credit card so that you have recourse in case anything happens, and you've signed contracts putting every agreement about goods and services in writing—and that's great. However, those steps won't get your money back if something unforeseen happens.

Imagine the worst-case scenario: Your wedding and reception have to be canceled because one of you falls ill; your wedding gown or his custom-made tuxedo is lost or damaged; a hurricane or other bad weather requires you to postpone the wedding; one of you is called up for active duty; a vendor doesn't supply your wedding cake; the wedding rings are lost or damaged—any number of things could go wrong. Now imagine that you are financially protected in the event that one of these things disrupts your wedding day.

If you're having the wedding and reception at a private home, you might want to get insurance in case someone is injured or there is damage to property. Although a homeowner insurance policy may cover such incidents, it's best not to file a claim against it if you don't have to. Some reception sites require you to carry wedding insurance, so make sure you investigate this if you haven't already.

Contact your insurance agent for quotes or look up wedding insurance companies on the Internet. You'll have to decide if it's worth the extra money (possibly a few hundred dollars for a five-figure wedding), and you'll need to include the cost of protecting your investment in your budget. The more you spend on your wedding, the better idea wedding insurance may be.

95. Build Your Personal Wedding Website

A personalized website contains a variety of information about an upcoming wedding, including a story of how the couple met, photos, directions to the wedding site, and links to area attractions and events. Such websites can be quite creative: Sometimes couples share funny stories about each other or visions of their future together. Some feature a time clock to show how many days, hours, minutes, and seconds are left until the "big event."

Visitors to a website can R.S.V.P. online, let the bride and groom know what entrée they prefer at the reception meal, advise them of any special needs, find out at which hotel the wedding party has a group rate, and leave messages. Putting up a Wed site means you don't have to repeat the same information to all of your guests individually.

As a bonus, a wedding website enables you to save money on sending everyone pictures of the wedding and the honeymoon. You can upload digital pictures to your website immediately. You can even post a streaming video of your wedding for friends and family who missed it in person.

How Much Do You Spend to Save?

Prices for hosting your website will vary widely. Some are free, and others will run you more than a hundred dollars a month. Some sites require you to be a techie to set them up. Others are slick, easily assembled templates that require little from you beyond typing in some information and uploading pictures. Here is a list of popular wedding website hosts:

- *www.myevent.com* charges a small monthly fee to host your wedding website. You supply them with information about your wedding, and they will create a website for you.
- *www.ourperfectday.com* provides all the services you need to create a wedding website for a small fee. You choose colors and fonts, supply information and photographs, and let someone else design and maintain your site.

- *www.theknot.com* is a free website service. You choose a design and add details about yourselves and your wedding day. Add-ons are available for purchase.
- *www.ewedding.com* is another free web service that offers snappy, professional-grade designs and multiple options for sharing news about your special day with your friends and family.

CHAPTER 21

Budgeting for Pre-Wedding Parties

The wedding day isn't the only celebration. From engagement parties to bridal showers to rehearsal dinners and morning-after breakfasts, there may be a flurry of pre-wedding parties that can be thrown for you. Even though you're not the hosts, you should still encourage your loved ones to seek ways to save money on the plans. Share the wisdom from this book, and ask them to keep the following additional tips in mind.

96. Build Your Guest Lists

For every party, keep the guest list small. Engagement parties don't have to involve everyone who will be invited to the wedding. Just a handful of close friends and family are all that's

193

usually invited. For bridal showers, the guest list will often be larger, so party planners will need to put multiple budget-savers into action. The rehearsal dinner can include only the members of the bridal party and their dates, your relatives, siblings, and the officiant, plus anyone who is performing a reading. You don't have to invite all out-of-town guests to this event if you're on a budget. That trend is fine for those with unlimited funds, but you don't have to follow suit. The morning-after breakfast can include just your families and the bridal party, and perhaps your out-of-town guests. As a breakfast or brunch, it's going to be an inexpensive affair.

Plan Couples' Parties

Couples' parties are gaining in popularity. They are a memorable way to get both the groom's and bride's friends together, regardless of whether they know each other already.

For a couples' party, a wine-tasting event appeals to just about everyone. Check to see whether there is a winery near you or consider having the wine tasting at a restaurant. A wine tasting is surprisingly affordable since guests are only tasting various wines. This is a classy party theme that makes a festive couple send-off.

Plan for Lower-Budget Catering

Having a party at a restaurant or having it catered are two easy alternatives if your budget permits. It's best to work out a set menu if you're having a meal in a restaurant, because it'll save on the price and lessen aggravation. No one wants to get mad at Uncle Bert because he orders lobster when everyone else is being careful of your budget.

Ask the restaurant whether it has sample set menus that have worked for other events and discuss how you want alcohol offered. If you haven't eaten at the restaurant before, be sure to stop by and sample the food in advance of choosing the venue.

The caterer you hired for your wedding-reception meal may also provide you with your rehearsal meal or other pre-wedding party meal. The advantages are obvious: You've already checked out this person or company and feel good about their service and food, and you may be able to work out a better price if they see they can get more business from you. Just make sure that the meal served for the rehearsal is sufficiently different from the reception meal.

For pre-wedding parties, the trend is toward more casual meals, such as a cookout in the backyard, or a family-style pasta dinner served at the dining room table. With everyone gathered, an informal celebration is often best, considering the more formal wedding to come. Caterers can meet your budget needs, especially when you ask for more casual arrangements. Again, check out the menu money-saving tips mentioned earlier in this book, and bring in the cake and drinks tips as well!

97. Plan an At-Home Party

More couples are choosing to have their engagement parties and rehearsal dinners at the home of their parents or a close relative. The location allows for more control over the menu. You can avoid pricey menus found at restaurants and catering halls, and you know what you can prepare in your own kitchen.

Hosting a party at home gives you the perfect built-in reason to keep your guest list small. You simply cannot invite a large number of people to your small-sized home. So you've had to limit your guest list.

You can set up a buffet on your dining room table, and move the dining room chairs to different areas of the house as natural seating areas. You may need to rent some chairs and extra wineglasses, but these expenses are small.

Homeowners who are proud of their outdoor decks and terraces often hold the parties out there, showing off their new deck décor, table and chairs and grill. Outdoor entertaining is a top trend for at-home parties, in a style that naturally saves money (as long as you're not grilling lobsters and steaks).

Hosts also say that they can provide enough wine and liquor from bottles they already own, perhaps bottles they received as holiday gifts. They don't need to spend hundreds of dollars on a fresh supply of liquor.

Décor need only be minimal, since you won't have a lot of guest tables for centerpieces to grace. Perhaps just one floral piece in the foyer and smaller collections of flowers on end-tables means you'll spend less than $40 on floral décor.

For entertainment, you'll simply turn on your CD player or iPod dock and play your own tunes. If there is a piano at your home, perhaps someone would do you the favor of playing a song.

BRIDAL BONUS As an added savings with regard to timing, there's no rule that says the rehearsal dinner has to be at dinnertime. If you're having the rehearsal earlier in the day, make it a lunch or afternoon event for less.

98. Explore Your DIY Options

Save money by making as much of the food as you can, and save time and stress by keeping the menu simple and using shortcuts. Like barbecuing? Buy chicken when it's on sale at the grocery store, and stash it in the freezer. Brush on a homemade or bottled barbecue sauce and serve corn on the cob and pasta salad. Dessert? Serve apple pie or order a cake filled with ice cream and decorated with an icing picture of the happy couple.

If you don't cook much or you're uncomfortable preparing food for a crowd, visit *www.allrecipes.com*. The website lists collections of recipes, enabling you to choose the type of food you want to serve.

Explore inexpensive catering options if you don't want the hassle of cooking for your guests. Many grocery stores and delis provide a catering service allowing you to reserve dishes ahead of time.

Want something casual and inexpensive? Set out a buffet of sliced meats and cheeses from the deli with an assortment of breads and rolls, cold salads, lots of pickles and olives, and condiments. Add several types of fancy ice cream and sherbet for a refreshing finish to the meal.

Want a more elegant occasion? Whip up several fancy entrées or casserole dishes, such as a chicken-asparagus gratin or beef burgundy. Prepare and freeze them in advance, then thaw them in the refrigerator the day of the rehearsal. When you arrive home, serve your guests some simple appetizers or a tossed salad with several types of dressing while the casseroles heat. If there is a French or Italian bakery in your area, fancy bakery cookies make a tasty but budget-conscious dessert.

A buffet is easier on the hosts than a more formal sit-down dinner, but caterers and other food professionals will tell you that people will eat more food when they serve themselves from a buffet. Be sure to plan for this if you want to have a buffet!

If you're part of a family that loves to cook, a potluck dinner can be a wonderful idea for your rehearsal dinner. Take this opportunity to connect with your culinary heritage.

In the weeks before the party, have one person keep a list of who's bringing what so you don't end up with too many desserts or entrées. Ask guests to write out the recipe for their dish and make enough photocopies for sharing. The happy couple can start their married life with a notebook of treasured family recipes, and other guests can have copies of recipes they admire.

CHAPTER 22

Finding Honeymoon Savings

Honeymoons can be expensive! Especially if you're paying for the wedding, you're probably concerned about the type of honeymoon you can take, the location, how long you can stay there. But you'll be happy to know there are terrific travel deals out there, and especially terrific honeymoon packages that might allow you to eat and drink for free!

99. Research Locations

The first step in planning a honeymoon is establishing your honeymoon style. This is especially important if you and your fiancé have never traveled together before. It helps to know at the planning stage that you are a beach bum while your fiancé is a museum-hopping globetrotter. Recognizing such differences ahead of time will help you plan a honeymoon that pleases both of you.

Sit down together one evening and do nothing but think about that honeymoon. Make sure you and your fiancé agree on a honeymoon style; you may have to incorporate a bit of each person's dream vacation to come to a happy medium.

Planning a wedding six to twelve months ahead of the date gives you enough lead time to do some honeymoon pricing. The farther ahead you make those airline or train reservations and book that room, the more you'll save. With at least six months to plan ahead, you have plenty of time to research the web for vacation ideas as well as bargain prices.

Make sure your travel agent is a member of a recognized professional organization such as the American Society of Travel Agents (703-739-8739, *www.astanet.net*), the National Tour Association (606-226-4444, *www.ntaonline.com*), or the U.S. Tour Operators Association (212-599-6599, *www .ustoa.com*).

Finally, check out what kind of weather is usual during the time period you'll be honeymooning. There's nothing worse than arriving in the Caribbean for two weeks of sun and sand only to have to turn around because a hurricane is bearing down on your island. Look into the weather and then make sure you have travel insurance.

Decide Where to Go

The Caribbean remains a hot destination with honeymooners. Jamaica, the Bahamas, Mexico, and St. Lucia are all favorite locales. Hawaii and Florida are popular tropical honeymoon locations in the United States. Las Vegas, New York, and San Francisco are prime sites for city-oriented honeymooners. Visit *www.honeymoonersreviewguide.com* and *www.travelandleisure.com* for details on many locations. You will find surveys and ratings showing the best budget beaches, for example, or the best budget resorts, which may guide your decisions.

Bridal websites also list their best bets in honeymoon locales, and the websites of major hotel chains report on the newest honeymoon packages, including freebies for the bride and groom.

Don't forget about your local AAA office, which is a wellspring of destination ideas, and with your membership discount, you may be able to get big savings.

Time your honeymoon for a site's best rates. Call a hotel directly, because a hotel chain's toll-free operator might not know about special deals relevant to the hotel you're interested in. Also visit *www.hotelcoupons.com*, *www.hoteldiscounts.com*, or another website that offers similar services to get information about special deals.

Honeymoon Tips

- If time and money are short, consider a "minimoon." Take an abbreviated honeymoon at a nearby locale to get away. This will still give the two of you a chance to be alone and relax after the stress of planning a wedding.

- Play the honeymoon card. Many people are happy to help newlyweds celebrate. Ask your airline ticket agent for an upgrade to first class, and let the hotel check-in clerk know how much you'd appreciate a room upgrade. Even if officials can't accommodate your wishes, at least you will have tried.

- Check visitor's bureaus and tourist organizations for lists of hotels and motels, as well as bed-and-breakfasts, where you might be able to stay on the cheap while being in walking distance to terrific shopping areas, beaches, and other attractions.

- Compare the price of a rental condo with other types of accommodations. Some people prefer these because they can cook an occasional meal, or do a load of laundry. Timeshares are also a great way to go on a honeymoon for less, so look into timeshare associations to see if this deal would be great for now and for your future travels.

- Stretch your budget by not booking the best room in the best lodging in your location. After all, you're sure to be out and about so much, you won't care that you don't have the most deluxe accommodations. Reserve a portion of your budget for that unexpected special restaurant you spot or a gift you just can't resist in a little boutique you discover. Remember to set aside money for tips and unexpected expenses.

- Leave for the honeymoon during your air carrier's lowest rate period (usually midweek).
- Establish a honeymoon registry so that guests can give you the gift of a special dinner, spa treatments, scuba diving expeditions, winery tours, and other fun elements of a romantic honeymoon. Your guests might even agree to split the cost of airfare or your hotel suite, or get you an upgrade!

100. Go Off-Season

Try to plan a vacation in the off-season. This strategy can save you money and aggravation. You'll also have more of the place to yourself to enjoy. One caveat: This doesn't work if you have your heart set on seasonal activities. If you want to go skiing, a June honeymoon in Aspen wouldn't make you happy.

How do you find out the peak season for a travel venue? Just ask! Call the travel venue or visit its website. You can also contact a travel agent or check a travel guide, search online at the travel websites mentioned earlier, and look at travel magazines for their roundups of the best seasonal locations and resorts.

Be aware of the "shoulder season," which is the period of time between peak-season and off-peak season, the transition weeks when things start slowing down a bit, prices are lower, but all of the area attractions are still open. You could save 20 to 40 percent on your honeymoon just by visiting in the shoulder season.

Steer clear of festival times, when resorts boost their room rates, restaurants charge more for meals and drinks, and the entire town is in bedlam. Ask the tourism department for your chosen location if there are any big festivals planned for the week of your visit, and decide if you want big savings . . . or the perk of being where the action is. You might decide you like a repeat of your spring break getaways in the past . . . but most likely you'd rather save a few hundred dollars by choosing a different location. Many festivals do take place during the off-season so that more rooms are available for their revelers, and to inject some needed tourist dollars into the local economy.

101. Go All-Inclusive

Consider an all-inclusive package, which means that all of your meals and drinks are included in the one price you pay for the week. Anything you want to eat or drink is already paid for, so you don't have to count the $12 drinks you're sipping by the pool or share a dessert because you've found it's a whopping

$20. Especially in the Caribbean, resort food and drink prices can be astronomical, so an all-inclusive deal may be your best bet.

There is a catch, however. When you look at all-inclusive prices, you'll see that the daily average for food and drinks is $90. What if you would never eat or drink that amount? It could be better for you, if you're not a big drinker, to just go à la carte, paying for $6 soda and $12 salads for lunch. You may have to do a little bit of math, but you'll be well rewarded for your efforts.

Resources

For information on everything you need to know about every aspect of planning a wedding, start with the wedding magazines and wedding vendors. Here's a list of some popular wedding websites:

 www.theknot.com

 www.brides.com

 www.weddingchannel.com

 www.TodaySBride.com

 www.MarthaStewart.com/weddings

www.wedfrugal.com

www.blissweddings.com

"The Dollar Stretcher" newsletter, available on *www.stretcher.com*, is a good source of money-saving ideas and suggestions from cost-conscious writers and contributors.

There are many websites offering coupons and rebates on wedding items. One popular site is *www.coupon.com*.

To find a class near you, check out your local adult-education or community-education departments, community colleges and four-year universities, county extension departments, YMCAs and YWCAs, and so on.

At *www.celebrityweddingsonline.com*, you can take a peek at the vows favorite celebrities used on their important day (actually, since most of them marry often, it should be days, right?). Choose the vows used by Kurt Cobain and Courtney Love, members of The Beatles, Julia Roberts, and more.

Better Homes and Gardens Creative Collections magazine often features helpful tips for weddings at home and in the garden. Its website is *www.BHG.com*.

Brides.com is the website for *Brides, Modern Bride,* and *Elegant Bride* magazines. Save time and money finding local vendors and sharing money-saving tips on the forum. Don't pay to have a wedding website set up; the site shows you how.

Martha Stewart's website, *www.marthastewart.com*, has hundreds of articles and photos to help you save time and money on your wedding and on making your first home together. Check out the budget tips.

Financial expert Suze Orman's website has eye-opening articles on the dynamics of money in a relationship. Read them at *www.suzeorman.com*.

The Knot (*www.theknot.com*) features an online budgeter to keep you on track and counts down the days to your wedding for you. Brides can personalize their budgets and find local resources.

Wedding author Sharon Naylor's website offers articles on wedding budgeting, plus worksheets to determine additional ways to save, *www.sharonnaylor.net*.

Smart Couples Finish Rich author David Bach's website is *www.finishrich.com*. Bach has written bestselling books on financial success.

Find great recipes at *www.foodtv.com* and *www.allrecipes.com*.

Find tourism departments anywhere in the world at *www.towd.com*.

Index

Index